Always "bee" your best!
Blessings —
Helen Halle

Bumblebees Fly Anyway

Defying the Odds at Work and Home

Thelma Wells

with Jan Winebrenner

First published in the United States of America in 1996 by WRS Publishing, a division of WRS Group, Inc., 701 N. New Road, Waco, Texas 76710
Book design by Georgia Brady
Jacket design by Joe James

10 9 8 7 6 5 4 3 2 1

Library of Congress Cataloging-in-Publication Data

Wells, Thelma, 1941–
    Bumblebees fly anyway: defying the odds at work and home / Thelma Wells with Jan Winebrenner.
                p.   cm.
        ISBN 1-56796-121-5
        1. Afro-American women—Life skills guides. 2. Afro-American women—Psychology.   I. Winebrenner, Jan. II. Title.
E185.86.W437   1995
305.48'896073—dc20

                                                                95-40728
                                                                CIP

DEDICATION

Many heroes and heroines have played a significant role in my life. This book is dedicated to the memory of my uncle and aunt, James and Allene Morris, and to the future success of my grandchildren, Antony D. Cox, age thirteen, and Vanessa Christtell Wells, age ten weeks.

CONTENTS

FOREWORD

I first met Thelma Wells on stage, where she was getting ready to sing for the National Speakers Association convention in Atlanta. She was to be the featured music, and I the speaker. When Thelma opened her mouth and began singing "His Eye Is on the Sparrow," I forgot what I had planned to say. In fact, I changed my entire presentation. Instead of the prepared speech I had brought with me to the podium, I began speaking from my heart, following Thelma's lead, and sharing with the audience the importance of my faith and the deep personal significance of the words Thelma had just sung.

Somehow, that day, Thelma's presence and the power of her musical message seemed to call out of me something more than I had planned on giving.

That is the essence of Thelma Wells. That is what she does best. She calls on us to exceed our own limitations, to go beyond the expected, the routine, the ordinary in all our pursuits. Because that is what she demands of herself.

Thelma was the illegitimate daughter of a crippled seventeen-year-old, and her birth was not greeted with great expectations. Growing up in an age governed by segregation and Jim Crow laws, she had little reason for high hopes. For years, she was subjected to discrimination, disappointment, and many other obstacles. Thanks to a godly great-grandmother, she was never embittered or overwhelmed by limits others might try to impose on her.

Even though she appeared to have had two strikes against her at birth, Thelma's been hitting home runs ever since. Her story is one of faith, commitment, courage, and a never-say-die attitude. It will inspire you to reach beyond your limits and give you some workable guidelines to help you do exactly that.

As she always does, whether singing or speaking, Thelma inspires and instructs, and she does it with heart and passion.

As you read her book, you will find yourself believing that you too can be the best of what you want to be.

That's Thelma's message—one she has not only spoken, but also lived. As you read it, I hope you'll be challenged to join her in the pursuit of excellence and the search for the best in yourself and in others.

—ZIG ZIGLAR
Author of *Over the Top*

INTRODUCTION

What would life be without heroes? What would we do without the stories of men and women whose achievements set an example of courage and a standard of excellence to which the rest of us can only aspire? As a youngster, I read books about my heroes, people like Booker T. Washington, who established the Tuskegee Institute to offer vocational education for black Americans during an era when blacks were denied the most basic educational experiences.

As I grew, I read and reread the stories of Marian Anderson, the first black to join the Metropolitan Opera in New York. Her talent was recognized internationally, but in her own country, she was refused permission to sing at Constitution Hall because she was black. I listened to the magnificent recordings of opera diva Leontyne Price who, because of the struggle of Marian Anderson, became a member of the Metropolitan Opera in 1961. I reveled in the joy of her success.

Music has always been my first love, so many of my heroes were musicians, like Mahalia Jackson and Nat King Cole, but that didn't stop me from being an adoring fan of Joe Lewis and Jackie Robinson. As I matured, I added more heroes, like Madame C. J. Walker, the first black woman millionaire who gained her fortune by producing beauty aids. In recent years, I've read books about the heroism of the black soldiers who served in World War II, giving their lives abroad while back home, in the country for which they were fighting, their lives were consigned little value. I've read of Maya Angelou and Rosa Parks and Barbara Jordon, and many others who continue to display courage and leadership for ordinary people, people like me.

As I've read the final pages of these books and closed

the covers, I've felt awe—awe that such men and women have graced my life, if only through ink and paper. And I've felt extreme gratitude that their stories live on in books that I can share with my children and grandchildren and my friends.

You can imagine then, that when I was asked to write a book, my first response was an immediate, "What? Me?"

People who write books have something of profound importance to say, I thought. People who have accomplished great things, people who've risen against all odds and achieved the almost impossible. People like Rosa Parks.

Well, I'm no Rosa Parks, I thought.

I'm ordinary. My life, like yours, has been marked by difficulties and a few achievements, but to write a book about it? What can I say that is significant and original? What can I say that deserves to be preserved? Whatever struggles I've encountered have been small, private ones. My victories have been few and mostly unnoticed, except to a handful of friends and family members.

My life has been ordinary by comparison to most. But the times, ah, now, those were extraordinary. Since my birth in 1941, the country, the world, has witnessed extraordinary events, events that have formed a fascinating backdrop against which commonplace, ordinary lives appear colorful.

Against the backdrop of the Jim Crow laws, against the scenery of the civil rights movement, against the horror of Vietnam and the end of the cold war, against the torn curtain that realigned Europe, and against the crumbling of the Soviet regime—against all these national and international landscapes, ordinary people like me have gone about the business of living. We have dreamed our dreams and charted our paths, knowing obstacles would arise to deter us. We've faced difficulties in our homes, in our neighborhoods, and in the workplace. And most of us have pushed through, refusing to be thwarted in the pursuit of our goals. Because that is what ordinary people do, every day.

I'm honored to tell a story that most ordinary folks will recognize as *their* story. Few of us are heroes. Few of us make noise that can be heard down the block, much less echo down the long corridors of history. It is our cumulative voices that are heard as we raise them together, crying out against injustice or heralding good news.

Each of us has a story to tell. As I tell you mine, I am reminded of a quote I read recently:

"It is our duty as men and women to proceed as though limits to our ability do not exist. We are collaborators in creation." (Teilhard de Chardin)

To proceed as though limits to our ability do not exist... To collaborate in creation... In the creation of opportunities, in the creation of relationships, in the creation of change and progress in our careers, in our communities, and in the larger world.

Such proceeding is not limited to heroes and valiant warriors, although we take courage from their valor, and we press on, remembering their tenacity.

Such collaboration is not reserved only for the supertalented, the superathletic, although their visible examples compel us to keep on trying, to keep on pressing against the limits until they give way and let us proceed onward.

As you will see as you read my story, the most ordinary individuals can ignore the limits and proceed one step at a time toward their goals. Even the most ordinary among us can collaborate in the creation of opportunity.

That is the theme of this book. It is about pushing past the limits that others would impose on us. It is about refusing to limit ourselves. It is about collaborating—with education, with people, with our own inner strengths and personality types—to create opportunity and change.

As you read these pages, I hope you will see the accomplishments of an ordinary woman, and will believe in your own ability to achieve and succeed. I hope you, too, will push against the limits and begin the work of collaborating in creation.

IT IS OUR DUTY AS MEN AND WOMEN TO
PROCEED AS THOUGH LIMITS TO OUR ABILITY
DO NOT EXIST. WE ARE COLLABORATORS IN
CREATION.

—TEILHARD DE CHARDIN

CHAPTER 1

THE FLIGHT
OF THE BUMBLEBEE

The lights in the theater dimmed. The feature was about to begin. I twisted in my seat to look up at the tiny projection window placed high in the wall near the ceiling. Lint sparkled like sunlight on a river as the flickering light flowed over my head and down toward the white screen below. I climbed onto my knees and stretched my arms through the darkness to let my fingers play with the dancing particles.

"Sit down, Thelma."

My grandfather's hoarse whisper was loud in my ear. The whirring of the projector hummed even more loudly. I plopped down in my seat, my chubby legs dangling, my eyes wide with the excitement of an afternoon matinee.

It was 1949. I was eight years old. And there was no place I'd rather be on a Saturday than in the Majestic Theater with my grandfather, Daddy Lawrence.

On many a Saturday, Daddy Lawrence and I joined the line of Negroes waiting to buy tickets at a window marked "Colored." Clutching Daddy Lawrence's hand, I walked with him through a doorway marked with a sign that read "Colored Only"—a side door, far away from the main entrance where the white moviegoers entered. Once inside, we walked quickly toward a roped-off area and climbed the stairs to the mezzanine. It was called the "buzzard roost" in those days, and coloreds who wanted to see a movie at the Majestic could sit up there, or nowhere.

"It won't always be like this, Thelma," Daddy Lawrence used to tell me when we stood in line to buy candy and popcorn and cold drinks at the separate concession stand

1

built upstairs to segregate us from the white customers downstairs. "Someday you'll be able to go wherever you want to go. Someday you'll be able to sit wherever you want to sit."

Throughout the movie, if the coloreds in the buzzard roost laughed too loudly, a white patron from the floor beneath us would shout, "Shut up, niggers! You're too loud. We'll put your black ass out of here!" Sometimes, the kids around me felt brave and tossed candy wrappers and bits of ice down on the white folks below and then collapsed low in their seats, giggling softly when they heard the startled outbursts from underneath them. It was small revenge, but my grandfather wouldn't allow me to take part.

"You show respect, Thelma. You want respect, you show respect. Things'll change someday, I know it. Things'll change."

Nearly forty-five years later, I walked into the refurbished grandeur of the Majestic Theater and stood for a moment in a wide doorway on the ground floor, my high heels deep in the plush of new carpet. I glanced at the ticket I held, and a young man in a tuxedo leaned toward me and spoke softly, "May I seat you, ma'am?"

I handed the usher my ticket and followed him down the center aisle to my seat on the second row. As the lights dimmed, I glanced over my shoulder and up, up high to the buzzard roost behind me where well-dressed theater patrons, black and white alike, had taken their seats and now awaited the orchestra's opening theme. On the stage, only a few feet in front of me, the heavy swathe of curtain swung aside and costumed actors stepped into view. The show began, and I was close enough to smell the greasepaint.

Things *have* changed, Daddy Lawrence, I thought, as I looked around me.

It was 1994. I no longer had to buy a movie ticket at a window marked "Colored." I could go where I wanted to go and sit where I wanted to sit. The Jim Crow laws had been wiped off the legislative books.

The doors that had been closed to Daddy Lawrence had swung open for me. Courageous individuals had pounded on those doors until the wood splintered and the doors fell off their hinges. And now I, Thelma Wells, could walk freely into any building. The "Colored Only" sign had been removed, replaced with one that read "Opportunity."

Back in 1949, Daddy Lawrence had steadfastly believed that change would come. But could he really have believed that one day it would be possible for his granddaughter, a black, illegitimate female child, to own a prosperous, bustling company? That Thelma Wells would one day travel the globe and be welcomed into five-star hotels and seated at the best tables in lovely restaurants? That I would make my living talking to people, all kinds of people and all colors, about being the best they could be?

That night, seated in the elegant Majestic Theater, I wished Daddy Lawrence could have lived to sit on the second row. I wished he could have seen the changes he had only dreamed of. I had only recently returned from an international conference in Germany, and the exhilaration of that experience was still fresh. The thrill of it still reverberated inside me.

I, Thelma Wells, of Dallas, Texas, had addressed a crowd of thousands gathered to celebrate Free Enterprise Day. The audience, composed of men and women from many different nations, represented nearly every race on the planet. My topic: How to be the best you can be.

Speaking through an interpreter, I had talked about how to succeed, how to achieve goals, how to define dreams and how to fulfill them. As I did often in my speeches, I used the bumblebee to illustrate my points and motivate my audience.

"The bumblebee isn't built for flying, you know. The odds are against it every time it spreads its too-shallow wing span," I said. "But every time it lifts its too-heavy body into the air, it defies those odds. And you too can defy the odds. You can be the best you want to be. Like the bumblebee, you too can accomplish what seems impossible."

The bumblebee illustration is my favorite theme. It has become a kind of touchstone for me, perhaps because its unlikely flight so closely resembles my own.

3

I was thirty-eight years old when I first heard that the bumblebee should not be able to fly, and I felt an instant affinity for that ill-assembled creature. According to the law of aerodynamics, it is built all wrong. Its maiden flight should have ended with a call to "911." Its species could be named *Insect titanicus*. No one really knows why it is able to get lift-off, but it does. And every day, millions of these doomed creatures take to the air while scientists and engineers of the world shake their heads and say, How do they do that?

Many motivational speakers have pointed to the bumblebee as an example of defying the odds, accomplishing the impossible and the implausible. You've heard the metaphor, probably many times before. Perhaps it has become clichéd, almost trite, for you. But for me, it is always fresh and vital. All I have to do is review my life, and the cliché becomes profound and profoundly personal. Like the bumblebee, I don't appear to have been assembled for "flight." All the typical elements associated with success appear to be missing, or at least poorly arranged, in my life.

Like the bumblebee, I didn't come into the world equipped to fly. That was the perception of a nation in 1941, the year I was born. Nothing about my birth suggested anything but a future of disappointment. In the eyes of a racially segregated culture, I was doomed by my race, my gender, and the circumstances of my birth. What could I expect to gain from life? What could I hope to achieve?

Who in their right minds would have believed it was possible for me to someday own my own business and travel the world, speaking to corporate executives, sales staffs, and office personnel about achievement, success, and personal job satisfaction? Certainly not I.

As a youngster growing up in Dallas, Texas, I never expected to become a motivational speaker. I never imagined myself standing in front of the employees of major international corporations, instructing them and sharing principles that would enable them to become valued employees and satisfied, fulfilled human beings. And yet, here I am. And what an amazing journey it has been.

Like any journey, it is filled with landmarks, like the afternoon matinees at the Majestic Theater. And it is filled with people, people like my grandfather, Daddy Lawrence, and many others who made the way easier, clearer—and others who at times made it almost impassable. But always it has been an adventure. And when I look at where I am today, I am astounded. I am excited. Because I know that if *I* have been able to find a route that will lead toward success, then others can too. Many others.

If you press me for a formula for success, you'll find my fingers straying to the gold bumblebee that I wear pinned to my lapel at all times. Humble, malformed, the bumble*bee* still represents for me the vital steps necessary for achievement:

B 🐝   Be aware of who you are and what you are

E 🐝   Eliminate the negative elements and influences in your life

E 🐝   Expect the best of yourself and of others

But beyond any formula or any cute cliché or acrostic, the success I have achieved can be best understood through a story. It is a story of people—people who loved me, people who challenged me, people whose paths crossed mine in a myriad of ways. Each of them walked alongside me for a time; some of them hoped to see me fall, some hoped to see me fly.

Come share my journey in the pages of this book. Our first steps travel through the neighborhood that was my first home—a four-square-block region in the city of Dallas, Texas. Meet the caring people who first instilled in me the values of family, friendship, and community.

CHAPTER 2

BABY GIRL MORRIS

I lied to Grannie for the last time when I was nine years old. It was a silly lie, and an obvious one, but I was a child, and it seemed reasonable to me to protect myself from danger. And when I disobeyed, Grannie was dangerous. Ferocious. A stocky-built woman, she was dark-skinned and strong. Strong enough to wield anger like a terrifying weapon.

I was a chubby child, far too chubby for my age and height, and fearing for my health, Grannie took me to the Children's Hospital for an evaluation. It was almost too late. An exam revealed dangerous amounts of fat deposits around my heart, and I was put on a strict diet. No sweets of any kind. The day I lied to Grannie, my chin was streaked with dark smears and chocolate puddled in the corners of my mouth, but I looked up at her and said, without blinking, "No, Grannie, I didn't eat any sweets."

"Girl, don't lie to me," Grannie growled. "You tell me the truth. You been eatin' candy?"

"No, ma'am," I murmured, looking up at her where she stood on the stairs that led to our garage apartment. She was looming over me, her eyes flashing like the fire under a skillet.

"What's that stuff in the corner of your mouth?" she said, taking a step toward me where I stood alongside the stairway.

I licked my lips and wiped at my chin with my fist.

"Girl, I told you not to lie to me... " Grannie was coming faster now, kind of crouched-like, swiping at me like a panther at her cub. Quick as I could, I darted toward the neighbor's house, Grannie's voice chasing me all the way.

"Don't you ever run from me, girl!" she hollered.

I ran faster.

"Child, you'll have to come back to this house sometime, and when you do, I'll be here!"

I heard the screen door at the top of the stairs slam shut as I scrambled into the brush of an empty lot not far away.

Grannie was right. I would have to go home sooner or later. On any other day, I'd have been glad to go home. Home to Grannie and Daddy Harrell, my great-grandparents. They'd raised me since I was a toddler, and no one loved me better than they did. Grannie's huge, heavy arms could pull me into a hug that was as tender as it was tight. At night when I crawled into bed with her, she told me stories and stroked my face and wrapped me in a cocoon of safety and security. When she laughed, her voice rumbled and her massive bosom shook like an earthquake. But when I did her wrong, she lost all humor.

I waited a short while before daring to come out from around back of the garage apartment next door and slink home. I pulled a couple of skinny switches off the big tree growing near the apartment stairs, and then I hauled myself up the steps and into Grannie's smoldering presence.

Sobbing, I handed Grannie the switches and then followed her into the bathroom. She sat down on the closed toilet seat and commanded, "Bend over."

"If you'll lie, you'll steal," Grannie said, panting, as her hand brought the switches down on my backside.

"And if you'll steal, you'll kill."

She said it again and again.

"If you'll lie, you'll steal, and if you'll steal, you'll kill."

The litany seemed never-ending, and so did the spanking. I could hear my great-grandfather calling from his post outside the bathroom door, "That's enough, sweetie, you've whipped that girl enough... that's enough!"

But Grannie didn't stop.

"I wanna trust you, girl, but when I catch you in a lie, that means I can't trust you."

Her heavy arms bore down on my fanny while she kept up the barrage of words.

"Always be truthful—even if it hurts. You tell me the

truth, girl. If I don't like it, I'll deal with it. You're too important to lie."

The spanking ended, and Grannie walked out of the bathroom and said not a single word for what seemed like days.

With Grannie there was no mercy. No mercy and scant forgiveness, and that only after sufficient suffering. We were Baptists, not Catholics, but Grannie believed in penance, not grace. And when I sinned, she exacted her due from me.

Grannie was as good a preacher as any alive, and she didn't wait for Sundays or a pulpit. I was her congregation, and every situation was an occasion for a sermon.

"We don't have much, girl, all we got is our name, but you always protect your name," she said.

"A man's word is his bond," she told me. "Keep your word, say what you mean, and mean what you say."

When I wasn't in trouble, Grannie's sweetness was like pure syrup. And although I feared her, I loved her dearly. I was about two years old when she and Daddy Harrell took me into their home.

Seventeen years old and unmarried, Dorothy Nell Morris was little more than a child herself when she gave birth to me on March 31, 1941, in the back room of her parents' home at 3010 Webb Avenue. In scribbled handwriting, she wrote "Baby Girl Morris" on my birth certificate.

A stroke in the early hours after her own birth had left my mother partially paralyzed on her right side. She carried her withered right hand pressed up against her breast, and her crippled foot gave her a sort of halt-drag gait, but her left side was strong and her will indomitable. Insisting on being independent, she moved out of her parents' home when I was an infant and took me with her to live in the servant's quarters of a wealthy white household in Dallas's Belmont addition.

I came to live with my great-grandmother and great-grandfather, Sarah and William Harrell, about two years later, when both my mother and I became very ill. Grannie asked if she could keep me until I was well. She took me to live with her and "Daddy Harrell" in the garage apartment, and I never left.

"I'll let you keep my child," my mother told Grannie, "but I'm not givin' her to you."

She may not have "given" me to Grannie, but I knew it was where I belonged.

Grannie made sure I went to see my mother often during my childhood, but after each visit, I was always more than ready to return to the garage apartment. I especially remember one overnight stay when I was about eight years old. My mother no longer lived and worked in the lovely Belmont home. Her days were spent in a small laundry, and at night she went home to a tent on Starks Street in South Dallas where she lived with my half-sister, Sarah. Tangled in gritty sheets spread on a small cot, I cried and stared at the dirt floor and recoiled in horror as skinny, mewing cats climbed over me, swishing their tails in my face.

I wanted to go home to Grannie and Daddy Harrell, to the tiny garage apartment. It was only five rooms—a living room, kitchen, parlor, and one bedroom with a tiny bath—but a screened porch opened it to the world. It was clean and safe and had a real floor. Nothing could have persuaded me that the apartment on Thomas Avenue was not my rightful home.

I loved my mother. She was sweet and loving toward me, and as I grew older we developed a very tender closeness. And Sarah, well, Sarah was everything a little sister ought to be—funny, and fun, and at times irritating— and over time we grew into great friends and confidants. And my mother's parents, Daddy Lawrence and Mother Dot, were always part of the scenery of my life, but during my early childhood, "home" was the garage apartment where Grannie and Daddy Harrell lived.

Daddy Harrell and I were the best of friends. Grannie worked as a domestic for a wealthy white woman named Mary Less, and Daddy Harrell looked after me until I was school age. He was blind all the years I knew him, and as soon as I was old enough to learn my way around the neighborhood, I became his eyes. Every Sunday I walked him to church. Often, during the week, I held his hand and led him down the street to Tapplet's Fish Market, or to the doctor's, or to visit his friends, or to the church.

One of my favorite after school games was "prayer meeting." The little parlor of the garage apartment became the St. John Missionary Baptist Church. The old sofa was a pew and a tall-backed chair the pulpit. Together, Daddy Harrell and I sang the old metered hymns of the church and hollered out long-winded prayers. Daddy Harrell sang with more enthusiasm than talent, but he could remember every word of his two favorites, "When the Battle Is Over We Shall Wear a Crown" and "I Shall Not Be Moved." His slightly off-key baritone wavered alongside my loud, childish voice. Together we belted out songs and prayed down fire and brimstone in our make-believe church.

Sometimes, on hot afternoons, we walked to the little variety store on Hall Street. "Pooch," Daddy Harrell would say, "Let's you and me go on down and get us a cold drink, shall we, baby?"

Daddy Harrell's death, when I was seventeen, was a terrible loss.

I stood on a grassy corner of Thomas Avenue recently and surveyed all that used to be my childhood home. From the vacant lot where my great-grandmother's apartment used to stand, I could look across a field and see the Crescent Hotel, one of Dallas's landmark buildings. I closed my eyes, memories roaming the familiar streets of my childhood. Remembered sounds of our once-bustling community enfolded me with wistful arms.

As a little girl, I had wandered down these streets, glancing into barbershops, beauty shops, dentists' and attorneys' offices, and medical practices, all owned by my black neighbors. I had waved at Mr. Bodden, the cobbler on the corner, and called greetings into the shops and offices where merchants and secretaries and doctors and lawyers all watched my comings and goings every day. If I passed by later than usual, someone always knew. Someone always scolded, shouting at me, "You get on home now, girl. What you doin' bein' so late today? Your folks will be worried now, you hear?"

It had been many years since I had thought about the people of my childhood neighborhood, but now I wondered about them all. What had become of that fine black matron, Mrs. Charles Etta Jones? She had been the executive vice president of Excelsior Life Insurance Company, and she had owned the house next door and several other properties as well. And what of Mrs. Strickland, who had owned the house on the other side of the garage apartment? Crazy, we used to call her when she came out of her house wearing long, flowing garments and head rags. But if she was crazy, she was also astute. Astute enough to earn a living off of her property by turning it into a rooming house. Colorful, accomplished people walked the sidewalks of my neighborhood— educated men and women who had attended Fisk University, Lincoln University, Bishop College, Wiley College, and other outstanding Negro universities. People like Mrs. Love, who had lived on the other side of Crazy Mrs. Strickland. People like Dr. Jordan and Dr. Williams and Dr. E. Homer Browne—people whose medical and dental clinics, whose homes and legacies of effort and determination now lay buried under soil, razed to make room for city expansion in the shadow of the Woodall Rogers Freeway.

They are all gone now, the people and the houses and the businesses. But what a community we once were! Dominated by the St. John Missionary Baptist Church on the corner of Allen and Gilluiott, the entire neighborhood often gathered in the huge red brick, colonial-style church. It was a central gathering place for many of the black citizens of Dallas. Pastored by Dr. Ernest Coble Estell, Sr., the church was not only our spiritual mecca but also the place where we heard sermons on the importance of education and community. In the early fifties, when black educators were not allowed to attend meetings held during American Education Week, Dr. Estell hosted teacher convocations in the sanctuary of the St. John Missionary Baptist Church and scheduled education seminars.

I'll never forget one of the first weddings I attended in that grand red-brick church. Autherine Lucy came to Dallas to get married. I still have pictures of her in her white silk dress. But the most treasured picture I have of her is the one I can only imagine. She's standing in a doorway at the University of Alabama, defying the governor who shouted, "No Negress will ever attend this school." On the day of her marriage, journalists and photographers, white and black alike, came from every corner of the country and waited outside the church to catch a glimpse of the brave young woman who had defied the governor's decree and dared to break the color barriers.

These were the people of my community, of my childhood. They were quiet people. Courageous people. I watched them, day after day, living lives that preached values more powerfully than a Sunday sermon. Some of them, like my mother, came and went on the fringes of my life, making sacrifices that I wouldn't fully appreciate until I had children of my own.

CHAPTER 3

A WATCHING COMMUNITY

My father, Robert Smith, was a simple man who worked as a meatpacker. He and my mother never married, but the woman he did settle down with made sure he remembered he had a daughter named Thelma. On or near the holidays, he came to visit me at Grannie's and brought us a ham.

A tall, good-looking man with an athletic build, my father was soft-spoken and gentle. He always seemed shy and a bit uncomfortable around me—but not so his mother. My grandmother Sophie Lipscomb Walton adored me and made sure I knew it. "Mother Sophie" was a tall, handsome woman with a stately manner. She was widowed while still a young woman. For more than forty years she worked in the home of a prominent Dallas doctor. His children and grandchildren called her "Aunt Sophie," but I was her only grandchild.

Although she earned her living as a domestic, Mother Sophie had the spirit of an entrepreneur. She turned her large, two-story home into a boarding house and earned a comfortable income from it. Proud, bossy, and vivacious, she was as flamboyant as she was intelligent. She always wore large-brimmed straw hats decorated with bright colored flowers and ribbons, unless it was her Sunday to serve as deaconess. On those Sundays, she traded in her showy straw hat for a demure white one to match her white dress and shoes and gloves.

Every week Mother Sophie phoned me and we chatted about my school work and friends and her activities at the Mt. Horeb Baptist Church.

"I had to talk to the mission society this week, and my, you should have seen those folks sit up and listen to me," she'd say. "I was *so* good today, child."

Prissy and proud, Mother Sophie collected compliments like souvenirs. She'd shrug, give the wide brim of her hat a caress, and answer, "I know, darlin', I'm wonderful. I do look good today, don't I?"

Phone calls and visits to Mother Sophie's boarding house gave color and texture to my life. She was one more person who cared about me and gave me significance. She was one more person who assured me that my life mattered.

The streets of my neighborhood were filled with people who cared about me and the other children who ran up and down the streets. There were dozens of us, and each of us was known to Mr. Bodden, the cobbler, and the shopkeepers and the others whose store fronts and offices opened onto Thomas Avenue and its adjacent streets. There was little we could do that wasn't seen by someone who would be sure our misbehavior was reported and punished.

I was a nine-year-old walking down the street one day wearing my best ruffles and bows, when a sleek black Cadillac with a set of longhorns on the hood pulled up alongside me. The driver leaned across the seat to roll down the window and offer me a ride. Curious, I glanced at him and kept walking. He stopped the car and said, "Hey, little girl, come here."

Shrugging, I took a step toward the glossy-looking car and leaned on the door to look inside. I hadn't had time to speak even a syllable to the stranger when I heard a woman's shriek. I looked up to see Althea Hilliard flying out of the dental office where she worked, hurtling herself toward me.

"You get yourself away from here, girl!" she said, heaving and hollering, "And don't you ever let me see you hangin' on this car or talkin' to this man again, you hear? Not this man or any other man, understand?"

She was squeezing my arm and her face was so close to mine I could feel her hot breath. I stammered, "Yes, ma'am."

"You don't talk to anybody and you don't get in anybody's car, not *anybody's*, you understand, girl?"

I nodded, my lip trembling.

"And you," she said, turning to the man in the car. "Don't you ever let me catch you talkin' to this girl again!"

Her voice rose until I thought everybody in the neighborhood would hear. Cringing, I tried to pull as far away from her as I could, but she kept a tight grip on my chubby arm while she screeched at the stranger. "You don't want to find out what I'll do to you if I ever see you around here again!" she threatened. "And you know I mean it!" she called out as the big black Cadillac drove away.

Althea bent over me and shook a skinny finger in my face. "You know what happens to girls that get into that man's car?" she asked me.

"No, ma'am," I whispered.

"Well, they get into all kinds of trouble, young lady, and you don't want that kind of trouble."

"No, ma'am," I said.

Althea finished her tirade and then let go of my arm, straightened herself and smoothed her hands down the front of her white hygienist's uniform.

"You do what's right, Thelma, 'cause I'll be watchin'," she said.

"Yes, ma'am," I murmured, rubbing my arm.

"And don't you think I won't be talkin' to your grandmother," she said, before she walked back into Dr. Browne's dentist office.

Sure enough, Althea talked to Grannie, and the lecture I got about talking to strangers and approaching strange cars had enough threats in it to make me vow never, ever, to be so foolish again. I learned that day that danger lurked in my neighborhood. Until then, I'd been oblivious to its presence in any form. It wasn't until I was older that I understood some of the men on our streets were "policy players"—gangsters and gamblers. But by the time I knew who they were and what they did, I was already aware of my many protectors.

Up and down Thomas Avenue, the neighbors watched the children. Mrs. Lola West kept an eye out from the front window of her house. Her son, Dr. Augustus West, observed our comings and goings from his medical office. And there were many others, but Mr. Bodden, the cobbler from the West Indies, was my most reliable guardian.

Mr. Bodden owned Bodden's Shoe Repair Shop on

Thomas Avenue. Every afternoon, he stood on the sidewalk near the doorway of his shop, wearing his dirty cobbler's apron and smelling of shoe polish and oil. From his lookout on the corner, he greeted the school children in heavily accented speech. Every afternoon I waved at him and said hello and then went on my way. When I reached the driveway that led to our garage apartment, I looked back to see Mr. Bodden still watching. After a nod and a final wave, he turned around and went back into his shop.

If I dawdled on the way home and passed the shoe shop later than usual, Mr. Bodden greeted me with a frown and a scolding.

"School's been out for half an hour, little girl," he'd say, nodding at the clock on the wall in his shop. "Why are you late? You go on, now. I'm going to stand here and watch 'til you get home."

The eyes of the neighborhood were always watching.

As a child, I didn't fully understand the importance of being watched over, being observed. But now, as an adult, I realize that my life was being lived in front of a community that valued its children. Mr. Bodden and Althea Hilliard and Mrs. West and Dr. West, and all the others who paid attention to the children of Thomas Avenue—they were telling us that what we did and how we lived mattered. It mattered not only to our families but to them, to the whole community.

The seeds of awareness were planted in those early years of my childhood. Awareness of who I was. Awareness that I was a small but valuable part of a whole. Awareness that what I did had consequences, not only to me, but to my entire community.

I was recently invited to speak to students in an inner-city high school where drugs and crime had reached epidemic proportions. "Be the best you can 'bee'," I told them, giving them the acrostic and the metaphor of the bumblebee. And then I asked them what their goals were. One by one, about half a dozen raised their hands and spoke up.

"I'd like to be a doctor," one boy said.

"I'm going to beauty school," a girl said.

"I want to be a teacher," another said.

And then, from the back of the room, a long arm stretched up over the head of a black youth. "I'm gonna be a drug dealer," he said, smirking at his buddy seated next to him.

He waited for my shocked response. I took a deep breath and, in a calm voice, answered, "If that's what you want to be, then be the best, but I'd like to talk to you about it."

The youth grinned and slouched down in his seat. Later, when the session ended, he swaggered past me and I grabbed his sleeve. "Let's talk," I said, pulling him into a quiet corner. "Tell me about your decision to sell drugs."

"It's about money, man," he said, shrugging. He was a tall, skinny kid with a handsome face and angry eyes.

I peered up at him and said, "That's your choice, but I just want to be sure you've got the whole picture. Have you thought about the negative side? The consequences?"

He shrugged again.

"Like prison, maybe an early death?"

The boy turned his face away from me.

"Tell me about your family," I said. "How about your parents? What do they think of the idea?"

He lifted a nonchalant shoulder and kept his eyes away from mine. He seemed to be staring at something ugly and distant. "Do you have a sister?" I asked.

"Yeah," he answered, and he let his eyes meet mine for just a fraction of a second.

"What if somebody tried to sell her drugs? What would you do?"

"I don't want her doin' drugs," he muttered, and his slouched posture stiffened.

"Everybody you sell to is someone's son or daughter, someone's brother or sister. Every drug you sell is a killer."

He shifted his gaze to the floor.

"Son, you can make your own decisions about your life—we all have to. But you have to be aware of who you are—you're a brother, a son, a young man with a future. But if you choose to deal drugs, you'll be dealing

in death. And there will be consequences. In your family—
and in my family."

The boy took a step away from me, but not before I
could put my hand on his arm.

"It matters, you know. It matters to me what you do
with your life."

Over forty-five years ago, Althea Hilliard had decided
that my actions were important to her. She had interfered
and she had made a difference. She had been there in
my neighborhood when a child took a step toward the
danger zone. She had interfered. She had made me aware.
She had made me see consequences.

Mr. Bodden, from the doorway of his cobbler's shop,
had interfered. He had stepped in to say he cared, if only
with a wave and an occasional scolding.

My family, Grannie and Daddy Harrell, and the other
neighbors and shopkeepers all up and down the street,
the ones who had watched from the windows and the
doorways—they all played a part in giving my generation
of children an awareness of who we were and how
valuable we were.

That day, after I addressed that roomful of students, I
wondered about their communities. I wondered who was
watching them, from doorways, from office windows.
Who was giving them a sense of community, a sense of
value, a sense of their identity as a part of the whole?

Was there a Mr. Bodden on their streets? An Althea?
And if not, what could I say or do to call them to
awareness of who they are? Each was a part of a whole. A
valuable piece of a community, each with something
worthwhile to contribute. Each was a child with abilities
and potential, if only someone would help them see it.

I wanted to make them aware that their actions have
consequences. I wanted to intervene. I wanted to rush
out to the curb, like Althea Hilliard did, and rail against
the dangers of the street. Was there anything I could say
that would convince an angry, too-thin kid in oversized
clothes that he is a part of my community and that his
life and what he does with it matters to me, that what
he does impacts us all, that consequences are far-reaching?

My upbringing was not traditional, my beginnings

inauspicious, but a handful of people who loved me communicated to me that my actions have consequences, that my life has value, that what I do impacts more than just myself. That's all it took—a handful of people.

Within my small, close-knit community, from the doorway of Dr. Browne's dental office to the stairs to Miss Charles Etta Jones's garage apartment, the message was articulated clearly: "You're a part of us, Thelma Smith, and we care about you. You behave yourself, because what you do affects all of us."

The message rang through our humble streets. I wasn't the only child who heard it. Dorothy Foat Coleman heard it. She's now a professor at UCLA. Fredie Cohen heard it—he teaches architecture. His brother Marion heard it—he's a supervisor for the Pacific Railroad. Gloria Foster Kirven heard it—she's a successful entrepreneur. Kay Frances Jones Thomas, a longtime teacher in the Dallas schools, heard it. Kathleen Reynolds Edwards, employed with the city of Dallas, heard it; Edwina Corney Cox Evans heard it—executive director of The Bethlehem Foundation.

A newscaster recently spoke of what he called the "sad plight of children of the streets." And I thought, *I* was a child of the street—in a sense, we all were, growing up on and around Thomas Avenue. But the streets were filled with neighbors and family, people who were committed to a community. People who took responsibility for one another and for one another's children. As children, we were nurtured from every doorway and every window.

Of the generation of children raised in that now-buried neighborhood bounded by Thomas Avenue, most have become productive, contributing members of their community. They were imbued with the belief that they were an integral part of a whole. They grew up with a sense of community and a sense of their place in it. Their lives are examples of what can happen when people band together to say loudly, "Consequences matter; community matters; our children matter to us."

I wonder, who is watching the children of your community? Is there someone, anyone, who cares enough to stand on the corner and call out a warning to the little ones who walk alone down dangerous streets?

Who is willing to care about the kid next door, the kid across the alley? Have we time to lean across the patio railing, or walk across the street to visit with a youngster who may not believe his life or his actions matter to anyone?

Dare we not take time to engage in conversation with a young person and listen to his dreams and his disappointments?

It takes only a few moments a day to make a difference in a child's life. But those moments, invested consistently, can create accountability in a youngster. They can create hope. They can create a sense of belonging.

A few weeks ago, I heard a young man pay tribute to a woman who had invested herself in his life. To her, the investment had seemed small, almost minuscule. As his Sunday school teacher, she had spent time with him each week, but it wasn't much. She had listened to his problems, problems with friends at school, sometimes with his parents. She had kept his confidences.

"She told me the truth," the young man said. "It wasn't always what I wanted to hear, but she wouldn't lie to me. She made me think about my life. She made me feel like I mattered, like I was important to her. That contact once a week, sometimes a phone call or a note in the mail, made me feel as though I was connected to someone who cared very much about my life and my conduct."

Embarrassed, the woman fidgeted in her seat while the young man talked about her in front of the Sunday morning congregation. She had never imagined that her small investment of time and interest would yield such a rich return. But here it was, in flesh and blood, the reward for her simple caring.

Of course, many factors play a part in the development of a young man's character, but on that day, one young man acknowledged that the concern and personal interest of one woman taught him lessons of accountability and inspired him to live a life of integrity.

Mrs. Hilliard and Mr. Bodden probably never foresaw the impact their unselfish interest would have on the little girl who lived down the street from them in a garage apartment. I was just one of the many for whom they took responsibility. Their example compels me to urge you to look around you, because you too can make a difference in a child's life. Consider your community. Find one or two youngsters you can encourage. Phone them. Send them notes and tell them of their value—to you and to their community. Convince them that their lives matter and their conduct has consequences. Convince them that, although no one else may seem to care, you do.

Grannie understood these things. She refused to let me go through life without experiencing consequences.

Althea Hilliard understood these things. She forced me to see that my actions mattered—not only to me, but to her as well. She made me aware of the importance of being accountable to a community that cared about me. I can still hear her high-pitched voice ringing in my ears, "You do what's right, Thelma, 'cause I'll be watching."

CHAPTER 4

"IF YOU'RE BLACK, GET BACK"

My childhood, while it is rich with memories of loving people who watched out for me and wanted the best for me, is also marked with vivid recollections of those who did not care for me. My grandmother, Mother Dot, was one of those.

I was a great source of embarrassment to my mother's mother. She was already embarrassed by her daughter's handicap, and my presence as an illegitimate child was an added humiliation. The fact that my skin color was very dark further confirmed my status as a pariah.

A perverse kind of caste system operated among the black community. Our people, conditioned by a segregated culture, had functioned under the philosophy that "if you're white, you're all right; if you're black, get back." Ironically, while this prejudice sent us into the back of the bus, it created a kind of bigotry among our own ranks at the same time. Because the white community treated light-skinned blacks better than those with very dark skin, it was not unusual for light-skinned Negroes to consider themselves superior to those with darker skin. Mother Dot, with her gold-toned skin, needed no convincing to believe that her dark black, bastard grandchild was an inferior creature.

In the black vernacular, Mother Dot was what we called a "high yellow." When I was a little girl, I thought she was an odd-looking woman. She wore her dyed brown hair shaped in finger waves that looked like huge apostrophes around her thin face. Lean and wiry-limbed, she was all bones and sharp, dangerous edges. Why she married sweet, gentle Daddy Lawrence, with his dark chocolate coloring, no one ever understood—least of all her mother-in-law. Grannie Harrell used to say of her, "That's a lotta yellow thrown away."

As a very young child, I sensed that Mother Dot resented me. To her, I was a burden to be borne—a dark-skinned reminder of her daughter's sins. But to her husband, Daddy Lawrence, I was a child to be loved.

Daddy Lawrence was a short, stockily built man with a soft voice and quick laughter. He worked for the Katy Railroad that ran from Knox Street to Union Station in downtown Dallas. On many occasions, I remember going down to the train station with him and boarding the train for a ride into the city. He lifted me up onto a seat and, shaking a finger at my nose, he ordered, "You stay put till we get to the end of the line, you hear?" Then he left the car and I rode alone, bouncing in my seat, listening to the clack-clack of the train, and pressing my face against the window to watch the city pass by. When I stepped onto the platform in Union Station, I was always amazed to see Daddy Lawrence there to meet me. How'd he get here before I did? I always wondered. It was years before I figured it out: he'd been in a front car, and when the train stopped, he'd hopped off and hurried toward the rear where I was riding. He was always there to greet me, grinning at me as I skipped toward him. He'd take off his narrow-brimmed cap and wipe his head with a handkerchief, smoothing the fringe of silky black hair that circled his nearly bald head. Then he'd swing me up in the air, and I'd wrap my arms around his neck and bury my face in the crisp fabric of his striped coveralls. The tangy scent of Old Spice cologne clung to his uniform and mixed with the smells of engine grease and dust and honest, hard work.

Such an unlikely couple, my mother's parents: he, dark chocolate in color and as gentle as a spring lamb, and she, an introverted, golden-skinned woman, easily angered and sparing no love for a child. Unless I was sure of spending time with Daddy Lawrence, I dreaded going to visit my mother's parents. Mother Dot ironed laundry for white families, and every day except Sunday, she set up her ironing board in the front parlor. If Daddy

Lawrence left for the day without taking me with him, she herded me into a narrow closet in the front bedroom.

"I don't want to see you runnin' around in here while I'm ironin'," she said, as she shut the door and closed me in the stifling darkness. "I don't need you gettin' burned by this hot iron." The closet doors muffled her voice and the sound of her footsteps as she walked away and left me.

It was a meager closet, pungent with the faint smell of mothballs and old wool. I huddled in a tight ball at one end of the floor clutching a blanket and let the darkness take me off to sleep. Hours passed before the door opened again—usually a short while before Daddy Lawrence was due to come home.

As I left childhood behind, I found ways to limit my visits with Mother Dot, and I outgrew the closet. It wasn't so easy to order a teenager into a dark, narrow closet on the pretext that she was in danger of getting burned by a hot iron. And I also learned that there were many different kinds of closets.

I was fresh out of high school, the ink on my diploma not yet dry. I was full of excitement about my future, and for good reason. Under the attentive eye of Grannie and the entire watching neighborhood, I'd completed my education with honors. I'd accomplished nearly every goal I'd set for myself. In elementary school, I'd discovered I could sing, and I'd found a platform for performing in my church. I'd won contests at school; I'd been in pageants and shows and talent competitions. My academic honors were numerous—every kudo a student could aspire to, I had claimed. I was confident and filled with anticipation. My community and my extraordinary family had given me a strong sense of identity and self-esteem. With the exception of Mother Dot, the people in my life had affirmed me and loved me. I was dating a wonderful boy named George Wells, and I believed nothing but joy and success awaited me.

The day after graduation, I phoned the registrar at the city's finest secretarial school to inquire about enrolling.

"Yes, we are registering students for classes," the voice on the phone told me. I caught my breath. "You'll have to come down to the school for an interview. How about tomorrow afternoon?"

I wore my best dress, a flowered print Sunday dress, and high heels that clicked on the sidewalk as I hurried toward the streetcar that waited on the corner. Holding onto my straw hat, I stepped up into the car and sat down in the closest seat. The ride downtown seemed interminable.

This is it, I told myself. It's finally going to happen. I'm going to secretarial school.

I'd had jobs during high school, little jobs after classes, like proofreader at the Excelsior Life Insurance Company and receptionist at the Henry Ford Realty Company. But this was the beginning of my trek toward a career. Nothing could stifle the excitement I felt that day.

The streetcar stopped at the corner of St. Paul and Elm. I climbed down, smoothed my dress, pressed my hat down firmly on my head, and straightened my shoulders. I walked the short distance down the street to the building that housed the secretarial school. Drawing a big breath, I stepped into the lobby and, moments later, I stood in the office of the registrar.

A bulky perspiring man with thinning blond hair sat behind a massive desk and squinted up at me through thick, smudged glasses. I swallowed and then smiled, but before I could say anything, he frowned at me and growled, "What are you doing here?"

"I called about applying to your school," I answered, my fingers fidgeting with the handle of my purse. "I have an interview with the registrar."

"Not with this registrar you don't," he said, getting up from his chair. Planting pudgy hands on his desk, he leaned toward me and snarled, "We don't accept niggers in this school."

I remember stumbling out of the building and peering up and down the street through tears, willing the street car to appear. Throughout the ride home, I fought to control the anger that boiled inside me.

It was 1959. Four years had passed since Rosa Parks had refused to give up her seat on that evening bus in Montgomery, Alabama. Dr. Martin Luther King, Jr., was a national figure; the civil rights movement was pressing forward, thrusting itself into the chambers of the Supreme Court. In my own hometown of Dallas, I had watched individuals like Peter Johnson and Juanita Craft, the youth director of the NAACP, forge ahead, stepping into leadership. But the Civil Rights Act lay in waiting five years in the future, and a young woman could be denied entrance to secretarial school simply because of the color of her skin.

I thought I heard the crashing sound of a closet door slamming shut, cutting me off, isolating me. But this time, it wasn't the action of a cruel grandmother. It was the result of a stubborn prejudice that refused to die, despite the efforts of many to kill it.

I arrived home crushed and despondent. Grannie locked me in her arms and crooned her love, just as she had since I was an infant. Then, when the tears had been wiped off my cheeks and all words of comfort had been spoken, Grannie got all businesslike. "Thelma," she said. "I thought you always wanted to go to college, not secretarial school."

"Well, yes, Grannie," I sniffed, "but where would we get the money for college? Secretarial school's a lot less expensive."

"If you want to go to college, God will make a way, don't you worry," Grannie said.

College? Could it really happen? I wondered.

The women in my family had never achieved a college education; however, some in my neighborhood had, including Mrs. Charles Etta Jones, the executive vice-president of Excelsior Life Insurance, and Mrs. Smith, who owned the Hill-Smith Hotel, and Mrs. V. Alyce Foster, who sold real estate. A few others were teachers and nurses, but the vast majority worked in the homes of wealthy white families, cleaning and cooking and serving. I wanted more from life than a maid's uniform.

Ironically, it was the wealthy white woman Grannie worked for who made it possible for me to attend college. Mrs. Mary Less had always been a kind and generous employer. Over the years, she had shown genuine interest in my education and my extracurricular activities. She had applauded my accomplishments and encouraged my every endeavor. When I was elected company queen of the ROTC ball, Mrs. Less had bought my ball gown. When I graduated third in my class, she sent her congratulations. When she learned of my longing to go to college, she called and asked me to come visit her.

"I understand you want to go to college, Thelma," Mrs. Less said, peering at me with intense blue eyes. "Is that right?" she asked. A middle-aged woman, Mrs. Less was small and slender and soft-spoken. Her pretty round face held a serious expression while she waited for me to answer.

"Yes, ma'am," I said.

"If you could go to college, where would you go?" she asked. Without pausing a second, I answered, "North Texas State College."

Denton was thirty-seven miles up the road, less than an hour away from home and Grannie. And George Wells.

We'd been together, almost inseparable, George and I, for nearly four years. I couldn't endure the thought of being too far away from him.

"Well, Thelma," Mrs. Less said, "you get a catalogue and tell me what you want to study. Then we'll talk again."

A week later, I went back to see Mrs. Less and told her I'd decided on secretarial science, a two-year program.

"If that's what you want, Thelma, I'll pay your tuition and buy your books," Mrs. Less said, "as long as your grades stay up and you don't get married while you're in school."

I tried not to gasp.

"If you decide to get married," she went on, "your husband will have to send you to school."

It was a generous offer, made from a kind heart. I accepted it.

Tuition and books, in 1959, was $475 per semester. Grannie agreed to send me spending money, about five dollars a week for laundry, snacks, and sundry needs. Daddy Lawrence committed to pay for my room and board. I had a little money of my own from part-time jobs I'd held over the years, but not much. My life-style would be severe, but the only thing that mattered to me was the classroom.

I could almost feel the swish of cool air as the closet door swung open.

I was going to go to college!

It would mean sacrifice—Grannie and Daddy Lawrence would be giving up much of their own small comfort to make this possible for me. But they would do it gladly, out of love.

Grannie had assured me that if God was in this plan, He would make it work. "God will make a way, Thelma," she used to say. I believed that then. I still believe it.

God does supply the fuel for positive changes in our lives. God is the author of all good things; He is the "Father of light," not darkness. And if He is on our side, nothing can hold us down.

As an adult, I've come to view the closet at Mother Dot's as a metaphor of life for many groups of people, as well as for individuals. Whenever I see closets opened and people released from the kind of situations that would confine them and isolate them, I remind myself that change not only requires God's help, but it usually demands sacrifice on the part of someone, or *many* someones. It may be the sacrifice of personal pleasure, it may be the sacrifice of a long-held prejudice. But change cannot occur without it.

I'm convinced of this: Change requires the power of God and voluntary sacrifices by individuals.

I saw these principles dramatically illustrated recently when a Fortune 500 company contacted me and asked me to meet with one of their local subsidiaries to try to resolve conflicts between white workers and black workers.

"That's not exactly what I do," I answered when the executive vice-president called from corporate headquarters in a neighboring state. Hadn't he read my résumé and my promotional materials? "Motivational speaker addressing issues such as customer service, employee self-esteem, cultural diversity." Nowhere did it say "referee."

"We believe you can do it, Thelma. Will you at least try?"

I wanted to say no—it sounded like an impossible task, but something wouldn't let me. So I gave an uncertain yes and began praying immediately.

"Lord, you know this kind of thing needs your power,

not mine. You've got to help me here. It's for sure I can't do this alone."

I began the process by meeting with the quarrelling groups separately, listening to their concerns and their complaints. I wanted to discover the truth. What was *really* happening in this workplace? Were the complaints valid?

There are always two sides to conflict. I learned quickly that the black and Hispanic employees perceived that they were hired for the grunt jobs; that if they happened to qualify for a more prestigious job within the company, the qualifications for those jobs were quickly changed so that a white applicant would be chosen; and that deliberate actions were often taken against them to build a case for their dismissal.

The white employees believed the black and Hispanic workers in the company were defensive, overly sensitive, and watchful for any slight, regardless of how innocent or unintentional. They perceived that some, or many, of the differences in treatment between whites and people of color were matters of policy, not matters of prejudice. And many white workers admitted that they had never associated, either socially or professionally, with anyone different from themselves.

My work was not going to be easy. Hostility vibrated in this workplace. I learned that a former supervisor had employed a management style of manipulation, intimidation, and verbal abuse that usually included racial slurs. Although he had left the company a few months earlier, his poison still hung in the air.

Months after that first phone call with the company executive, I was still meeting with employees, trying to discern the truth, trying to bring the two diverse groups together, trying to find a bridge of trust between workers. I discovered that some of what the black workers had believed was true. In several instances, job qualifications had been changed to give white workers the advantage in applying for promotions and in-house lateral positions. Complaints against black workers had been documented and placed in their personnel files without their knowledge, thus depriving them of an opportunity to correct a wrong or to learn from it—this, while white workers were informed of complaints, allowed to discuss them or rebut them, as well as change their procedures. Black workers had grown so sensitive to injury that they had imagined some situations and blown other incidents out of proportion. Many white workers had no knowledge of people with differences and had made no effort to get acquainted and find the similarities they share.

It was also true that some situations that were genuine policy matters had been mistakenly labeled racial issues. This further isolated employees and created still more hostility.

The issue, in the minds of the black and Hispanic workers, could be identified in one word: respect. While other workers, white workers, were treated with respect, allowed to work with dignity, the employees of color were not.

At times I felt overwhelmed by the task of resolving the conflicts in this company. I prayed often that the people involved would *want* to change, that they would desire not only a peaceful workplace, but authentic harmony between the races. And I prayed that the leaders in the workplace would set the example of sacrifice— that they would willingly set aside their petty prejudices, that they would give up their ideas of superiority and seek real change, on both professional and personal levels.

Changes began slowly as improved communication techniques entered the workplace. I encouraged managers to make great effort to treat all employees with the same degree of respect and to implement humor whenever possible—to "lighten up"—and to express appreciation often.

Feelings and behavior both began to change as workers agreed to try to consider situations from a professional point of view instead of taking things personally. This simple tactic defused anger and redirected attention off of personalities and onto problem-solving.

It was not an easy task to convince every worker that prejudice was a major problem in this workplace. And it was impossible to convince every employee to eliminate color and ethnicity as a reason for respect and fair treatment, but most were willing to try. And the defensiveness of the minority workers diminished as they were allowed to participate in meetings that addressed policies and procedures that had not been explained to them before. They began to feel as though they were finally on an even playing ground.

As the process continued, the majority of the white workers acknowledged that most of the complaints from the minority workers were valid. It was the white workers who listened, and *cared,* who helped assemble a list of recommended changes they knew were needed. The list was long and carefully tailored to the specific needs of this group of workers, but the basics apply to every situation where people of color are isolated for no other reason than the shade of their skin. And the changes are evolving slowly.

The process is ongoing. I continue to meet with the employees of this company on a regular basis. I speak often with the out-of-state executive who asked for my help. And I report the small victories: some in the company were truly appalled to know that the problems were so bad; many spoke up loudly to say they didn't want to be associated with such behavior. These are the doorkeepers, the men and women who watch and stand ready, refusing to let anyone be locked away from opportunity or interaction because of a misguided view of what is important, like skin color.

Within this company, change is occurring on both the professional and the personal level. A closet door is opening, inch by inch it seems. Men and women of color are stepping out into the sunlight, released from the isolation and confinement of prejudice. But for every door that swings open, many others remain tightly shut.

I recently returned from conducting cultural diversity workshops for a leadership conference for the criminal justice system in a southern state. The group consisted of prison wardens and other personnel who work with inmates in correctional institutes. It could not have been a more culturally diverse group.

Economic origins, social status, race—every difference that could separate and divide was represented among this group of leaders. They had assembled to address the issues that confront them in their workplace—prisons, correctional schools, probation offices—on a daily basis. Issues revolving around prejudice, hatred, violence, and every negative attitude and response imaginable had to be confronted. Individuals were to examine themselves for behavior and attitudes that could cause them to mistreat not only the inmates they dealt with, but also the diverse individuals who worked alongside them.

I considered this opportunity one of the greatest challenges of my career, because lately the idea of promoting, even discussing, cultural diversity has come under attack.

In recent months, America has begun to seriously question the rightness, the fairness of affirmative action and quota hiring. It seems as if a whole new wedge is being hammered down into the already dangerous division between the races. Somehow, the concept of cultural diversity seems to have gotten tangled in this net of controversy. It was my job to do what I could to cut it loose, to disentangle the confusing and confining threads of political rhetoric from the idea of cultural diversity.

My first objective was to emphasize this fact: Cultural diversity is *not* affirmative action.

It is not my goal to come into a company and tell them they need to hire more minorities. Nor do I consider it my responsibility to address the issue of quotas. The task I have taken for myself is to introduce the issues of dignity in the workplace; I do not address issues involving the EEO. My agenda is not political but humanitarian.

"Prejudice is as natural as drinking water," I said, letting my eyes scan the audience attending the leadership conference. Women, men, old and young, black and white, they sat before me already conditioned by life's experiences to respond to people according to the color of their skin. But they had gathered together with a sincere desire to move past the surface, to go deeper than the dermis, and reach into the heart of other human beings to find value and worth.

We would find that value together, by first discovering our sameness.

In a spirit of cooperation, the organizers of the

conference had asked each of the people attending to bring with them something from their homes, something from their past that represented who they are and what they are about.

I sat in wonder as a white affluent lawyer held up an expensive pair of running shoes.

"These represent where I came from. When I was a kid we were very poor. My first sneakers cost a dollar at a thrift store," he told the group.

A black man sitting near him nodded, remembering the poverty of his youth.

A white, middle-aged woman held up a picture of her family. She had married at fifteen years of age, had several children, and had lived nearly all her life as a wife and mother. Now, an employee in a correctional institution, she worked among girls who had given birth in their teens. She performed her job alongside women who, like her, had salvaged strength from small, hidden stashes and had found a way to preserve an ill-fated marriage. Around her, smiles of recognition creased the faces of a dozen women.

Others held up various items, all brought to reveal the person that lived beneath the layer of skin, whatever its color. One by one, men and women shared their stories and learned of their common origins, their common interests, and the values they held in common.

Emotion shivered through me as I watched and listened to these individuals tell about themselves. Together, we discussed the issues that united us—family, faith, ambitions and dreams, poverty, past hurts, and precious memories. Then, we turned our thoughts to the differences that tend to separate us—food choices, skin color, musical tastes, style, historical heritage. The differences seemed almost trivial, almost inconsequential, when compared to the deep significance of the things we shared in common.

Several people in the group spoke up to tell how the differences had enriched their lives. I watched as others nodded in agreement. A few voices murmured, "Yeah, that's right." Others smiled, remembering an incident when they had been enriched by interacting with those who are different from themselves. I could see eyes widening in surprise as stale, stereotypical images dropped away, and unique, valued human beings stepped into view.

At the closing session of the conference, I was overwhelmed by the show of appreciation and enthusiasm from everyone. Many spoke to me and to each other about a sense of commitment to respect the dignity of others without respect to skin color. With words of commitment came an acknowledgment of responsibility.

Later, as I boarded a plane to fly home to Dallas, I reflected on the four days I had spent with those highly placed leaders from the state correctional department. I felt a sense of awe for them. Theirs must be the most difficult job—to deal daily with the people and the events that most of us only see in a short fifteen-second report on the evening news. Ours is a celluloid relationship—we view the tape of the violence and horror—theirs is flesh and blood. We touch a button on the remote control and peace and quiet return to our world. The men and women I'd met that week could not turn off the scenes that play daily in their workplace. It was their job to get up every morning and face the day's headlines, delivered not in newsprint but in person.

I wondered if the goal of the conference had been achieved. Had we, together, been able to set standards for behavior and attitudes? Standards that would reflect respect for the dignity of every human being, regardless of skin color? If so, had we moved closer to the day when hiring quotas would no longer be needed? When we would no longer need to legislate fairness and mandate equal opportunities for every individual, regardless of color? When the EEO could be eliminated because men and women voluntarily exercised fairness and displayed genuine respect for one another, without concern for ethnic or cultural differences? The conference planners had asked me to explore the problems that exist because of racism and other forms of prejudice and discrimination. I'd done my best, calling on all my research, all my experiences, and every ounce of humor I possessed. I'd tried to show how much alike we are, while at the same time acknowledging our differences. Now I was going home to my world and they would stay in theirs, in the south, where roots of racial hostility still clung stubbornly to the soil.

What would be the outcome of four days spent focusing on how to foster the values of integration? Only God knows the answer to that question. The only thing I know is that the job is not complete. There is still much to be done.

We don't like to admit it, but there are still many dark places, closets where people sit isolated because of skin color, physical handicap, or other differences that aren't understood. Each of us must take responsibility for opening the doors and dispelling the darkness.

In your neighborhood, in your workplace, *you* can light the way toward justice and fair play. You can speak words of acceptance and encouragement. You can walk away when the bigot tells his racial jokes. You can refuse to laugh. You can help unlock the closet and release those who deserve the light of opportunity. In some cases, it may take a bit of urging and prying, but when the door finally does swing open, you will share in the exhilaration of those who, for the first time, are being allowed to pursue their dreams. You will experience the joy and satisfaction of having collaborated in the creation of meaningful relationships, as well as the creation of career opportunities.

I can't open a closet door without thinking of the child who once huddled in the darkness. That child is now a woman with a business of her own because someone opened the door and allowed her to step into the light of opportunity.

CHAPTER 5

"I LEARNED IN SPITE OF YOU"

I met George Wells at church when I was fourteen years old, and I said, "That's the boy I'm going to marry." Of course, I'd have to persuade Grannie to let me date him first—that was going to be a huge undertaking. Once that was accomplished, convincing her we should marry would seem easy.

Grannie didn't think fourteen-year-old girls ought to be out alone with boys. In that era, most folks agreed with her. Few of my friends and classmates were dating, so I didn't really feel Grannie was being unreasonable. But I did have reason to wonder if she would ever relent and let me go out with George, or with anyone, for that matter.

Once before, about a year earlier when I was barely thirteen, Grannie had agreed to let me go to a high school dance with a boy named Johnnie. He was a senior, and I was overwhelmed that he had asked me, a freshman, to be his date. Grannie had known Johnnie and his family for years, and if anyone was going to be trusted with her granddaughter, it was Johnnie. Of course, we had to agree to abide by her rules, which decreed that Daddy Lawrence would drive us to the dance and Johnnie's dad would drive us home. My curfew for the night was 11:30.

The dance was everything it was supposed to be. The gym at the old Moreland Branch YMCA was decorated with a spinning, mirrored ball that cast sparkling prisms about the room like tiny dancing stars. Girls wore oversized corsages pinned too high on the shoulders of full-skirted dresses and clustered in tiny cliques, whispering and giggling. Boys wearing too-tight ties and high-gloss polished shoes slapped each other on the back and gulped pink punch. Some couples danced while

39

others stood and talked quietly in dark corners of the room. Johnnie and I, shy and awkward with each other, danced a little and talked even less. When his father arrived to drive us home, we were both relieved.

The drive home should have been short. The gym wasn't far from the apartment on Thomas Avenue, but Johnnie's father suddenly remembered an important errand and decided to take care of it before he drove me home. I began fidgeting in the back seat, glancing at my watch, knowing we would never get home on time if Johnnie's father made a stop first. He was driving many miles out of the way, in the opposite direction of my waiting Grannie, and I wasn't only going to be late, I was going to be very late. I knew Grannie would show no mercy.

When we finally got home, long after the agreed-on curfew, Grannie was incensed. No amount of explanation would soften her anger. She'd been terrified—certain I lay dead in an alley somewhere, and nothing can stoke fury better than terror.

It didn't matter that I'd had no control over Johnnie's father. Grannie was too upset to listen or to be rational. For days, she refused to speak to me, and I suffered her silent fury until finally I summoned the courage to confront her.

"Grannie, this is so unfair!" I exclaimed. "It wasn't my fault, but you're punishing me as if I deliberately stayed out late and made you worry."

I watched Grannie struggle internally, then finally, as if weary of sustaining the emotions of anger, she let go. Shrugging, she nodded at me, and began discussing some mundane topic, acting as if nothing in the world had ever come between us. But I knew it would be a long time before she trusted another boy with her granddaughter's life and safety. It would be a long time before I was allowed to go out on another date.

My friendship with George began with phone calls, visits at church, and after school. Grannie liked him, which surprised me, and so did Daddy Harrell and Daddy Lawrence. The difference in our ages—George was seven years older—made Grannie a little nervous at first, but as she got to know him, it grew less and less important. She

40

didn't object to his coming over and calling me, and even seemed to look forward to his visits. By the time I was sixteen, Grannie agreed to let us go to the movies together if we had an escort. By the time I graduated from high school, George and I were inseparable.

George was a country boy, born and raised near Navasota, Texas. After high school, he had moved to Dallas to live with an aunt and uncle, W.D. and Doretha Cashaw. He had long harbored the desire to own his own company, and while I was finishing high school and thinking about college, he was working as an elevator operator in Mobil Oil's downtown office building. Watching for his opportunity, George made his plans and worked for his hourly wages, all the while knowing his destiny lay in a business of his own.

There were those who thought George and I were mismatched, and not only because of the difference in our ages: I, the scholarly girl, whose goals seemed high, almost out of reach, and he, the country boy with his entrepreneurial dreams that seemed just as unreachable. But George and I knew we were meant for each other. And that made it all the more wrenching when it came time for me to move to Denton and begin my studies at North Texas State College, as it was called in 1959.

Grannie and I had moved out of the apartment on Thomas Avenue a few months earlier. We had been approved for low-income housing in a project called Roseland Homes. For us, it seemed like a huge step up from the tiny upstairs apartment we'd lived in so many years, and, in many ways, it was a great move for us.

The "projects," only a few blocks away from Thomas Avenue and our many well-loved neighbors, was peopled by interesting, hard-working families. They were progressive folks, many of them blue-collar, but just as many were college educated as well. Many of my high school friends lived nearby, and it wasn't long before the new residence became truly home for us. The day I left for Denton I felt as though I was going to my own funeral.

"Why am I doing this?" I kept asking myself. "Is this really what I want? Is this really the right thing to do?"

The questions were no different than those being asked

by nearly every young person who is leaving home for the first time. The wrenching is painful, the uncertainties heavy. But underlying it all is a whispering call, saying, "Come—come! This is the direction of your destiny." I couldn't resist that call, no matter how many other clamoring emotions came close to drowning it.

In 1959, life at North Texas State College, for a Negro student, was very different than it would be today at any state college or university. Different, and yet in some ways, perhaps still somewhat the same.

Housing was a particular challenge for black students. If you were a black male athlete, the college had allocated special living quarters for you. On campus, Oak Street Hall had set aside one room to be shared by five black women students. A tiny room, too small for five women, it was next door to the boiler room. Whenever hot water ran anywhere in the dorm, the pipes in the next room clanged loudly. The black women in Oak Street Hall paid a price for the convenience of being on campus near their classes. They seldom studied in their room, and uninterrupted sleep was something they learned to live without.

If the one room in Oak Street Hall was full, black women students traveled to the community across the tracks and boarded with black families. My first year of college, I lived across the tracks in a house known to everyone as "the gray house."

Mr. and Mrs. Gray owned the gray, clapboard house that had been home to many black students over the years. I shared a room with two other girls also named Thelma, and two more girls lived in a downstairs room. One of them, Doris Crawford, became a lifelong friend. On the weekends, I traveled home to be with Grannie and George.

Campus life, for black students, meant total segregation from all social and academic activities. Besides being denied dormitory rooms, we were isolated from all sororities and fraternities, both social and honorary. We attended sports events and migrated toward each other, sitting together in our own sections, separate and distant from the white spectators. We created our own organizations and held our own parties and activities.

It was business as usual. I'd had no reason to expect life at college to be any different from life elsewhere for black Americans. I was accustomed to encounters that made me feel intimidated, isolated. But that was the way life was. Long ago I had learned that any encouragement, support, or sense of value I would ever receive would come only from the black community. It had always been that way. We built up one another. From the white community, we could expect nothing.

With the exception of Mrs. Less, who believed in me and was investing in my education, support and affirmation had come to me through my family, my church, and my school and community, which included no white people. Nothing in my experience had given me reason to expect acceptance or inclusion from the white student body at North Texas State College. And so I was not disappointed.

At times, however, I was terribly frustrated.

Mrs. Word taught shorthand in the business department. Throughout the semester, I sat in her class, took notes, studied arduously for her exams, and scored high grades. When she asked for students to read back their dictation, I volunteered often, but she refused to call on me. She refused to acknowledge my presence in her class. She refused to read my name during roll call. Sometimes I waited after class to ask her questions, but she walked past me, ignoring me, pretending she could neither see me nor hear me. The semester dragged by, and I forced myself to attend class, to do my homework, and to learn everything I could in that class, and when it was over, I had earned a high grade. But Mrs. Word hadn't seen the last of me yet. I enrolled in her class again second semester.

Nothing changed. For another four and a half months, the woman pretended I was invisible. She spoke not a word to me and continued to skip my name when she called roll. Every day I walked into class, determined to achieve, with or without the help of Mrs. Word. And I made up my mind that nothing she did would discourage me from learning shorthand, and learning it well.

At the end of the second semester, after the grades were issued and I'd earned a B, I went to find Mrs. Word. I was going to speak to this woman and make sure she heard me. I was going to make her acknowledge me whether she wanted to or not. I found her in her office one afternoon, and there was no way for her to escape me.

"Mrs. Word," I said, stepping up near her desk, "I just wanted to tell you that I learned a lot in your class."

Mrs. Word glanced up at me, frowned, then looked back down at the book on her desk. She couldn't pretend I wasn't there, but she wasn't about to accept my presence either. The best she could do was ignore me and hope I would go away. It didn't work.

"You're a very good teacher, and even though you didn't want to teach me anything, I learned a lot from you," I said, clutching my books tightly against my chest and speaking in a rush. "I know you didn't intend for me to do well. In spite of your refusal to answer my questions or let me read my dictation, I learned a lot. And I just wanted you to know that."

I breathed deeply and stepped back, watching to see what her response would be. Her eyes never looked up. Her mouth tightened, and in a sugary, sweet drawl, she told me, "I'm from Mississippi. I've never taught a Negress, and I don't intend to start now."

Barely able to control a smile, I answered, "I hate to disappoint you, Mrs. Word, but whether you wanted to or not, you did just that."

My first year of college ended, and I returned home to Grannie and our home in the projects. George and I began talking about getting married, and by the time I returned for my second year at North Texas, I knew we would soon be setting a date for a wedding.

During spring break of my sophomore year, I married George Wells. It was April 1, 1961, and the St. John Missionary Baptist Church was full to overflowing with friends and family who came to wish us well. My bridesmaids wore the pastel colors of spring, and in my white gown, I felt like the most beautiful girl in the world. I had never been happier.

Grannie and Daddy Lawrence made George promise to keep me in school until I graduated, and he agreed. I had changed my major from the two-year degree to a four-year degree in secondary education, so his commitment meant another year and a half of college, but he was willing and eager to see me finish school. We took a short honeymoon to San Antonio and Mexico, and when we returned, I went back to school, moving into Oak Street Hall while George moved into the house in the projects with Grannie. I came home on the weekends to be with my husband.

George's salary of $60 per week seemed like a lot of money to us. We had everything we needed, and even a few things we didn't need. Our life was moving in the direction we wanted, and it seemed as though every dream was going to come true for us.

My third year of college, I was back in Oak Street Hall again, living next to the noisy pipes in the boiler room. I hated it. I sought peace and shelter among the bookshelves of the library—no color barriers restricted us there. I could roam from aisle to aisle, research, read, study, and write letters to George without the hissing and clanging of water pipes. And without the isolation and segregation enforced elsewhere on campus. But I was happiest when I was able to go home and be with George. I thought I was dying when I had to return to school on Monday mornings.

"It won't be forever," George told me, week after week. "You're nearly finished, hon. Don't give up."

And week after week, I told myself the same thing, but every day it became harder and harder to stay focused. It became harder and harder to believe a college degree was worth this kind of agony. When George lost his job at Mobil Oil because the elevators were automated, I decided it was time to give up all this nonsense. One day, I packed all my belongings and came home, declaring to both Grannie and George that I wasn't going back to Denton.

"Oh, yes, you are!" George said. He picked up my bags, put them in his car, and drove me back to Oak Street Hall. I sniffled and cried all the way, but he refused to be moved by it.

"But what about the money?" I wailed. "What about your job? How are we going to afford it?"

"It'll be okay... "

"I want to be with you... "

"I know, Thelma, and I want you to be with me, but we're nearly there, baby. You're going to graduate in a year, and it will all be worth it... "

"I don't know," I whined, blowing noisily into a tissue.

"Thelma, I'm going to have my own business," George said. "Your grandfather and I are going to open a Mobil station. We've been approved for the franchise. You'll see, everything is going to be okay."

I stared at him, aghast.

"Your own business? Oh, George, I can't believe it! I want to be here with you!" (More wailing.)

"You're going back to school, and that's the end of it," George said. "I made a promise to your Grannie and to Daddy Lawrence, and I'm going to keep it."

We said a tearful goodbye in front of Oak Street Hall, but I never again tried to quit school.

Seven months after our wedding, I discovered I was pregnant with our first child. I moved home and commuted to school as a day student. Vikki was born on August 30, 1962, and Grannie and George agreed I should take a semester off, but by the following January, I was enrolled again, commuting as a day student, while Grannie helped care for our daughter. I graduated with a degree in education in August 1963.

A few months later, on December 21, 1963, I gave birth to our second child, a son. We named him George Fitzgerald Wells, in memory of John Fitzgerald Kennedy. One month earlier, we had mourned the death of the young president who had openly declared himself the friend of Martin Luther King, Jr. We had claimed any friend of Dr. King's as a friend of ours.

Politics in the early sixties were complicated, confusing. The civil rights issue had erupted like a boiling volcano, exploding suddenly after churning underground for a long, long time. Like hot lava spewing in many directions, the repercussions of boycotts and marches and militant standoffs spilled into nearly every community in the nation, purging, scalding, destroying, and redesigning the landscape of an entire nation. Scenes of Vietnam, a tiny country so distant, yet as close as the television screen in our living rooms, played around our consciousness, and all the while, the simplicity of friendship defined our politics. Who was for us? Who was against us?

CHAPTER 6

"MORE JUST LIKE ME"

Dr. Martin Luther King was a young preacher in his early twenties when I first met him. He had come to Dallas to preach at a Baptist Congress of Education, and along with several thousand people, I was excited about attending. The convention was held in the Memorial Auditorium, today's Dallas Convention Center. For this special occasion, the black population was to be given entrance.

I was a young wife at the time, preoccupied with establishing my home and career. I had never felt compelled to get involved in racial matters on a national level. I had never been an activist. But as I listened to the powerful words of Dr. King and felt his charisma flood the auditorium, I couldn't stifle a sense of excitement and exhilaration. He was talking about God's love for all men and women, regardless of color or station in life. He was urging people, ordinary people like me, to get involved in their communities, to work for change in nonviolent ways. The message rang pure and true. I felt a deep kinship with both the man and his message.

I shook hands with Dr. King that day and I thanked him for his words of encouragement. He would never remember me—I was one young black American among many thousands—but I would always remember him. It wasn't only his message—many African Americans I knew had said many of the same things. People like Grannie and Daddy Lawrence and the other quiet, diligent folks I'd grown up with had encouraged me and the other children of our neighborhood to do their best, to work hard, to live within the bounds of the law. But Dr. King had a visible platform from which to speak, and he had a plan. For the first time, during my era, the black community had leadership.

I felt hopeful that day as I left the auditorium. Hopeful that black Americans would see real changes. That America would see every citizen as a significant participant in the democratic process, regardless of skin color. I prayed that individuals of all races would learn to accept each other's unique gifts and allow each other to contribute and enjoy all the fruits of a free country, under God.

The curtain was being lifted on a national drama. I felt as though I was more of a spectator than an actor. Would there be a part for me, a young woman with a husband and children?

It was to be a small part, played out in my workplace and in the neighborhood where George and I would raise our family.

George had always hated living in the projects. For him, born and raised in farm country, the tiny attached apartments were like small jail cells. In 1963, shortly before our second child was born, we had the opportunity to buy a house in suburban Hamilton Park, and George couldn't wait to make the move. We packed our belongings and drove to North Dallas, taking Grannie with us. Together, we moved into the green house that would be our home for the next fifteen years, and I began working as a substitute teacher for the Hamilton Park School.

A totally black community, Hamilton Park had many similarities to the Thomas Avenue neighborhood where I'd been raised. Our neighbors were professional people—teachers, entrepreneurs, doctors, as well as "blue collar" workers. It was a healthy mix of families, and I became well acquainted with them through their children and through neighborhood activities.

Like the adults of my childhood home, I became a part of the watching community. I saw the children during school hours; I knew their schedules, their friends, and their activities. Soon, I was a younger, rounder version of Althea Hilliard.

Many "Altheas" lived in Hamilton Park. We all watched the children among us. Close-knit, caring, and quick to intervene if we sensed danger, we were a community of black families who knew that unless we helped ourselves and each other, there would be no help for us.

As a teacher, I observed a lovely phenomenon in the all-black school where I substituted. I saw black teachers, urgent about the task of teaching their own, investing themselves tirelessly to ensure the education of these children. I remembered my own years as a student in the segregated schools of Dallas, where the all-black faculty had a personal stake in our success, where they taught us with an intensity that cut through our boredom and made us care. These teachers were keenly acquainted with the obstacles that their students would face in the world of higher education and in the workplace. They taught with the goal of preparing these youngsters for those obstacles. They knew from painful experience how important a good education would be for these black children.

The Civil Rights Bill passed in 1964, our first year in Hamilton Park, and we celebrated with our friends and neighbors. But most of us knew that, while certain behaviors can be mandated by law, attitudes cannot. We knew that individual equality for most black Americans would be achieved in small increments, one step at a time, one encounter at a time—in the grocery store checkout line, at the post office, at the gas station, in the theaters and the real estate offices and the bookstores and the car dealerships and all the other places where short-term business transactions are carried out on a daily basis. But the larger battles against bigotry and prejudice would continue to be fought in the offices and warehouses and college dormitories and school classrooms, where people with differences would be forced to associate on a closer, more intimate level than ever before. In the South, where the divisions between the races had been drawn deeply and firmly for centuries, it would be especially difficult. After all, only a scant few years earlier we'd been drinking from water fountains designated "Colored"; we had been arrested for choosing a seat on a public bus or for entering a theater by the wrong entrance. The "Jim Crow" laws had served segregation in the South for many years. While they could be erased with a single swipe, they would not be so easily forgotten.

Certainly, the Civil Rights Bill would bring about changes, but brave, determined individuals would have to step forward and claim their newly legislated rights. And we knew that much of what would be gained would come in spite of great hostility. There would be a few who would welcome us into the workplace, into the classroom, into the community, as equals. But many more would resent our presence.

I knew all this, but I was ambitious, and as soon as I knew that Corporate America was open to people like me—a black female—I quit teaching and applied for a job in the business community.

It was an easy decision to make. I appreciated the teachers I worked with and I loved the children, but the corporate world lured me. I wanted to be a part of it.

In November 1964, I went to work for J.D. Enterprises (not its real name). They had advertised for a secretary with very specific credentials: The applicant must be black and female. I figured I was perfect for the job. I was hired after the first interview.

The southwest regional offices of this company had never employed a black person. Several northern offices were integrated, but the Dallas area was pure white. I understood from the start that my job was not simply to perform office tasks, although that might have been the job description on file. Certainly, much more was required.

As a "token," I would fulfill the mandates of the law, but I would also be responsible for doing everything I could to change the perceptions and the biases of the people with whom I worked. It was up to me, in that environment, to represent my people, African Americans, in such a way that negative stereotypes could be broken down and ignorant prejudices could be corrected.

I was hired to be a secretary, but when I reported to work the first day, I discovered that I had been assigned to the mail room. I tried to hide my disappointment.

"Be the best mail clerk you can be," I told myself as I dug into a huge pile of mail and began sorting it.

"Be the best mail clerk you can be, Thelma," I chanted, as I operated the foot pedal on the ancient addressograph machine.

Thelma L. Wells
Speaking at the 49th Annual Federal Safety and Health
Conference in San Diego, California
1995

Thelma Louise Smith at five
or six years of age

"Grannie," Mrs. Sarah Harrell,
the lady who raised Thelma

Thelma Louise Smith and her sister, Sarah Elizabeth Stinnett
(circled, right), with their cousins in the 1940s

HARPER STUDIOS

Graduation from Booker
T. Washington Technical
High School, 1959, as a
member of the National
Honor Society and third
in her class

Lawrence Morris, Sr.
Thelma's grandfather, "Daddy Lawrence"

Little Palace Eat Shop (above) and Hill Smith Hotel, two of the businesses on Thomas Avenue

DIAN MILLS

Mrs. Althea Jones Hilliard, the watcher in the community who reprimanded me for being lured to a man's car on Thomas Avenue

Thelma Wells in her "token" job at
J.D. Enterprises (not the real name
of the company)
1964

George Wells and Thelma Smith's wedding day,
April 1, 1961, at the famous St. John Missionary
Baptist Church. Daddy Lawrence and Grannie
(his mother) are in the background.

George Wells's Mobil service station at the corner of
Second and Grand in Dallas
1962–1973

Grannie (Sarah Harrell) holding Lesa Michele Wells the day
we came home from the hospital. Vikki Lynn Wells and
George Fitzgerald Wells pose for the picture.
May 29, 1969

Vikki Lynn,
Thelma's oldest child,
with her husband,
Edward Paul Newsome

George Fitzgerald Wells, Thelma's second child, with
his wife, Katrina L. Wells. Their daughter, Vanessa
Christtell Wells, (inset) May 7, 1995,
on her christening day

Antony D. Cox,
George's son and
Thelma's grandson
1995

Lesa Michele Wells Cohen, Thelma's youngest child,
with her husband, Patrick L. Cohen

Thelma's great-grandfather (William Harrell, Daddy Harrell)
and great-grandmother (Grannie Sarah Harrell)

Gloria Foster Kirven speaking during
Negro educators' celebration of American Education Week
at the St. John Missionary Baptist Church in the fifties.

Thelma's mentor, Mrs. Doretha Cashaw
(also the aunt of Thelma's husband, George)
1993

Mrs. Willie B. Johnson,
another of Thelma's mentors who actively
worked to improve the Hamilton Park
community in Dallas, Texas

Dr. Joseph Williams, Sr., Dr. Frank Jordan, Dr. E. Homer Browne,
at new office building at 2918 Thomas Avenue, Dallas
(Contributed by Mrs. Julia Jordan, widow of Dr. Frank Jordan)

W.L. LONG

Autherine Lucy's wedding
at St. John Missionary Baptist Church
1950s

Mrs. Mary Jo Evans,
who gave Thelma her motto:
"You can be the best of what
you want to be!"

Sarah Elizabeth Stinnett, Thelma's sister; Dorothy Nell Morris
Calhoun, Thelma's mother; and Thelma L. Wells at
Thelma's daughter Lesa's wedding
1993

NORTHPARK NATIONAL BANK PROMOTES THELMA WELLS

Thelma Louise Wells has been promoted from banking officer to assistant vice president of NorthPark National Bank, according to bank president, C. Thomas Abbott.

Ms. Wells joined the NorthPark National Bank in 1974 and is now head of the New Accounts and Certificate of Deposit Department.

Ms. Wells is a graduate of Booker T. Washington Technical High School, earned a bachelor of science degree from North Texas State University and is a member of the board of directors of the American Institute of Banking.

She is a member of the Bank Administration Institute, the southeast chapter of the Business and Professional Women's Club of America, Inc., the North Texas chapter of the National Association of Bank Women and St. John's Baptist Church. Wells is married to George Wells and has

MRS. THELMA WELLS

three children -- Vickie, Lynn, George Fitsgerald and Lesa Michele.

NorthPark National Bank is one of Dallas' fastest growing financial institutions with assets exceeding $133 million. The bank is located at Park Lane and Boedeker.

Newspaper article announcing Thelma's banking
promotion to assistant vice-president of
NorthPark National Bank in Dallas

Dr. Martin Luther King, Jr., and Dr. Ernest Coble Estell, Sr., at
the National Baptist Convention in the Dallas Convention
Center (formerly the Dallas Memorial Auditorium)

Thelma and George Wells
1989

"Be the best mail clerk you can be," I muttered, as I walked the hallways delivering envelopes and packages.

I smiled at my co-workers, memorized their names, and gave them all a cheerful wave when I made my pickups and deliveries. And always, I watched.

How did Corporate America dress?

What did Corporate America eat for lunch?

It was necessary to fit in, to assimilate. And so I observed and made changes to prove that my presence, the presence of a black person in the workplace, would not be a distraction. That we could blend into the work force, contribute our gifts and talents, and become an integral part of any company's success.

I noticed that the women usually wore skirts and blouses, so I added these to my wardrobe, saving my brightly printed dresses for Sunday church and other occasions—not to give up my own unique style, but so that I would be seen less as someone different, and more as just another employee. I didn't want to stand out as odd, nor did I want to completely abdicate my own identity, but this was a unique time, a serious time. It was a time to major on the majors. It was not a time for being distracted by smaller issues. My goal was to achieve excellence, and to do it without creating schisms between myself and the newly opened corporate environment.

Lunchtime was a particular challenge for me. My first day on the job I discovered that the company lunchroom was segregated—men on one side and women on the other. I decided to join the women. With a cheery hello, I sat down at a table and opened my brown paper bag and pulled out my sandwich. The other women murmured greetings, lowered their eyes, and acted uncomfortable. I could read their minds—What do you say to a black person?

Most of the people in this office were from working class families. They had never had a single conversation with an African American. If they had come from privilege, they would have had some association with blacks—a maid, a gardener, or possibly a cook. But these folks lived in middle– to lower–middle-class neighborhoods. When they thought of diversity, it was in terms of car manufacturers—U.S. or foreign made—or the color variety of aluminum siding available at Sears. Their neighbors were white, their children's friends were white. For most of them, Negroes were janitors, housekeepers, maybe athletes, and often convicts. But lunchroom companions? Not likely.

Only four years earlier, in a Dallas diner, a group of blacks had insisted on being served at the lunch counter. Their insistence grew to a protest, and before the day was over it had gained national attention. No longer would black Americans accept the rule that "colored" could not eat at a lunch counter where whites were served. Under Martin Luther King's leadership, more and more black Americans grew bold to resist the bigoted rules that enforced segregation, and over time, we had gained access to public places without fearing arrest. But most whites in the South were still uncomfortable with the presence of a black person in an eating establishment, unless he was the fry cook or the dishwasher.

Now, here I was, newly hired in an all-white company, and I had claimed a seat in this lunchroom. I glanced at the women around me and saw their heads drop and their fingers fidget with their lunches. I almost laughed.

They've said hello to a black elevator operator and probably told a black man to "fill 'er up," I thought, but they don't have any idea what to say to me.

So there we sat, together, uncertain, silent.

We're all women, I thought, with husbands and children. That ought to be a common point.

And so it began there, with small talk about kids and families. We were alike in one small way, it seemed.

But there was one major obstacle that loomed before me in the lunchroom. Tupperware.

All the white ladies at J.D. Enterprises brought their lunches in Tupperware. My brown bag had to go. But where did a black woman find a Tupperware party?

Growing up on Thomas Avenue, I'd never heard of Tupperware. And no Tupperware lady had ever tried to book a party in the projects. So what was I to do?

It was such a small thing, but to me it was very important. I wanted to meld into the social system in the company, eliminating as many "differences" as I could. I wanted the white people I worked with to learn about me, as a person, and to be able to say, Why, she's really no different than the rest of us. She's a woman, a worker, a human being.

I wanted a set of Tupperware.

Sometime during my first few weeks of employment with J.D. Enterprises, I noticed a television ad for a twenty-piece set of Tupperware. When the screen flashed a phone number to call "to inquire about a consultant in your area," I called immediately. A few days later, a Tupperware lady delivered·my twenty-piece set, and my lunchroom dilemma was solved.

I was now fully assimilated into Corporate America, or at least the lunchroom at the Dallas regional offices of J.D. Enterprises.

That step taken, it seemed nothing could block my climb up the corporate ladder. In January 1965, I was promoted to secretary to the parts manager.

I had proven myself—those first three months in the mail room had been the testing ground. Could a black person enter the workplace, work among whites, and not cause trouble? Could she pull her own weight? Could she do the job without triggering costly distractions among the other employees? Could the company afford to hire black workers? These were the questions I was supposed to answer, but I had a few of my own to ask. Would the company like the names of other black individuals who wanted to work hard and achieve success? Was the company interested in a few more black Americans just like me?

I knew many more black Americans just like me—fellow graduates of Dallas's Booker T. Washington Technical High School, college friends and neighbors—fine people whose skills perfectly matched the needs of J.D. Enterprises. They were educated, ambitious, and ready for the opportunity to contribute to and succeed in the corporate community. I gave their names to the different department managers as new hiring quotas arrived in the Dallas office. What a thrill it was for me when some of them were hired.

The presence of more black individuals in the workplace was, in some ways, both a triumph and a pleasure for me, but I also felt a very real sense of relief. No longer was I the "only one." No longer was I the token.

Before I was joined by other African American workers, I'd often felt like a laboratory animal in an experiment—an elaborate social experiment. People were watching me, studying me, observing my every move, and then analyzing the data and sending it on to be studied again by other eyes. At times, I found my co-workers staring at me with looks of astonishment, amazed to find that we were so much alike. To some, I knew I would always be viewed as an unwelcome alien; to others, like my college teacher, Mrs. Word, I would always be an invisible presence best ignored with the hopes that I would go away quietly.

I refused to go away, but I was often quiet, especially in the lunchroom, when the conversation strayed to racial issues.

"I think Martin Luther King is a communist," Lucy said to me one day over her meal of cold lasagna and green beans.

I felt a chill rattle down my neck, and it didn't have anything to do with Lucy's leftovers.

Lucy (not her real name) was as friendly toward me as any white woman was willing to be at that time, but I wouldn't have described us as friends, exactly. She didn't move when I sat down next to her at lunchtime, and she wasn't embarrassed to greet me in the hallways. Over our plastic ware, we'd had many conversations, but family and religion were our favorite topics. We both believed in love of family and God, so these were safe topics, topics we agreed on. On this day, however, it seemed Lucy felt safe enough with me to express some thoughts that might not be so agreeable.

"It makes me so mad," she said, shaking her head and frowning. "We were all doin' just fine 'til *he* came along and started messin' with things. Why'd he have to get everybody all stirred up?"

Timid, cautious, I stumbled about in my mind,

wondering how to respond. Don't cause trouble, Thelma, I warned. Don't kick up a fuss—this is your job we're talking about here...

"Uh, well, you know, Lucy, things weren't really all that fine for everybody... I mean, not everybody thinks we were *all* doing that well... "

Great, Thelma. Coward!

"Well, I still think he's a communist," Lucy said, snapping the lid shut on her Tupperware and then "burping" it.

Martin Luther King, Jr., a communist?

Blinking, I sat in silence, remembering the man I'd met and the words he had spoken. I thought about his manner, his methods, his goals. You're wrong, Lucy, I thought, but it was too late to say it out loud. Her high heels were already clattering across the cracked linoleum of the lunchroom floor.

She's gone, I thought, and almost gave an audible whew! But more than relief, I felt disgust.

What's wrong with you, Thelma? I thought. When did you start worrying about what other people are going to think of you?

What had happened to the fiery woman who had never been afraid of anyone except Grannie? I'd fought with people over less important issues. Since when had I grown shy about expressing my feelings? There'd been a time when I'd have wrangled with anyone about almost anything.

When had the fire in me begun to cool?

I knew the answer: when my paycheck became more important to me than my principles.

I had a bitter taste in my mouth when I went home that day.

And I vowed that I would challenge Lucy's thinking at the first opportunity.

For several days after that conversation with Lucy, I prayed for courage and wisdom. I wanted to speak up for the cause of black Americans. I wanted to defend the leadership and intent of Dr. King, but I wanted to do it without jeopardizing my job. My income was important to our family, and I had worked hard to secure my place at J.D. Enterprises. Did I dare risk it all? Was it my task to educate Lucy, or anyone else who didn't understand? Could I do it without appearing to be a troublemaker?

I found out a few days later.

"Did you see the news last night?" Lucy asked me as she sat down across from me at a table in the lunchroom.

I had seen it. Along with the rest of America, I had sat in front of my television set and watched as the governor of Alabama ordered troops to stop the march of peaceful protestors on their way to Selma. I had cringed and wept as I watched men and woman and children drop to their knees, choking on clouds of tear gas. I had fought nausea as I viewed troopers shouting and swinging billy clubs, forcefully trying to break up the marching crowd demonstrating for nothing more than equal voting rights for all Americans. Later that night, my sleep had been haunted by the images of attack dogs turned loose on men and women and children. I couldn't rid my dreams of the sight of men and women, gathered for a nonviolent protest, being assaulted and harmed by such deliberate viciousness. I'd awakened still troubled by feelings of horror and outrage.

"Frankly, I was glad to see it," Lucy said. "It's about time those folks quit all this protest foolishness. Maybe after having the dogs turned loose on them like that they'll stop all this business of protesting and marching. Like I say, I think it's about time."

Suddenly, the old fire inside me flared up and burned away all thoughts of cautious, well-chosen words.

"You're wrong, Lucy!" I blurted, rising out of my chair.

Suddenly, I didn't care if I was labeled a troublemaker. I didn't care if I was fired. I could no longer keep silent. I couldn't sit still and let the movement to which I was so indebted be so horribly maligned. And besides that, somebody needed to slap old Lucy with a wake-up call, and I figured it was going to have to be me.

"Lucy, I can't take this anymore! When I wanted to go to secretarial school a few years ago, the registrar wouldn't let me apply because I was black," I said. "I had a college teacher who wouldn't give me the time of day because she'd 'never taught a Negress' and she wasn't about to start now."

Lucy stared at me, speechless.

"It wasn't so long ago, Lucy, that I had to go around to the back door of a restaurant to order a hamburger, because my skin wasn't white. And there I stood, next to the garbage dumpster in the alley, waiting for my order. Can you imagine how that feels? And to have to get my drink out of a water fountain labeled 'Colored,' because I might contaminate the water for you white folks—do you really think that's okay, Lucy?"

Lucy swallowed and stared up at me, her eyes wide. There I stood, hands on my hips, flashing heat and flames, while poor Lucy gulped.

"I used to try to sneak a drink out the 'Whites Only' fountain, just to see if the water was any different," I said. "You tell me, Lucy, do you *really* think things were okay that way?"

I sucked in a deep, vibrating breath, before raving on. "Now, let me tell you this, honey, Martin Luther King *isn't* a communist, and I don't ever want to hear you tell me that he is. He's trying to make people like you understand that things have to change. You think this is a free country when black Americans can't buy a home they like, or apply for a job they're qualified for, or get an education to become *qualified* for a job?"

Lucy blinked up at me where I hovered over her. We were both shaking. She lowered her eyes and fingered the lid of her Tupperware.

"You watch Martin Luther King, Lucy. Do you see him with guns? Is he shouting obscenities in the streets? Is he telling people to riot and tear up the community?"

Lucy glanced up and shook her head.

"Is he saying we should throw out the Constitution?" And then I answered my own question, "No! He's saying we should uphold it, for all Americans. Is he telling people to get rid of the Bill of Rights?"

Lucy shook her head slowly.

"No, Lucy. Say it—NO! Martin Luther King is trying to get the country to enforce the Bill of Rights, to see that it isn't just for white folks, it's for everybody!"

My chest was heaving and my voice was strident. Lucy's mouth had dropped open and, just as she was about to try to answer me, I drew a breath and blasted her again.

"When he's arrested, does he fight back? And the people who march with him, are they violent? No, Lucy," I said, my voice trembling, my whole body shaking. "Martin Luther King isn't a communist. He's leading black Americans in nonviolent protests, because somebody has to do something to call attention to the gross inequities in our society."

My tirade was over. Lucy sat and stared at me, stunned and silent.

My throat burned and my lungs were gasping for air, as though I had just run the last mile of a marathon. I felt weary, yet exhilarated, exuberant.

I dropped back down into my chair, closed up my Tupperware and took a long sip of iced tea. Lucy got up quietly and left the room.

For several minutes I sat there in the lunchroom, aware of many pairs of eyes on me. My boss will hear of this incident within minutes, I thought. And then what?

Would there be a pink slip in my next pay envelope? Would I be reprimanded for being a troublemaker? Would my opinion, so vehemently expressed, be a reason for my termination?

I returned to my office and went back to work, distracted by thoughts of what I had done. Over the next few days, no one mentioned my outburst. On payday, there was no pink slip. There was no dismissal, no reprimand. I had said my piece and no one chastised me for it. In the southwest regional offices of J.D. Enterprises, it was business as usual.

It's been many years since that encounter with Lucy—an encounter I like to think of as the first of many cultural diversity workshops I've conducted. Of course, the curriculum has changed greatly over the years, and my communication style has improved, I hope. But the task of educating individuals about one another, the task of helping workers understand each other and accept each other's differences, is never finished.

The employment environment is ever-changing. Beginning in the early 1960s, it was the slow and steady flow of African Americans into the workplace—a strange and unsettling phenomenon for many white employers and employees. As more and more immigrants enter the U.S., the face of the American worker continues to change. But it is not only the work force that is undergoing change. The profile of the typical customer also is being revised.

In my workshops addressing cultural diversity, I often show diagrams of the changing percentages, the rising numbers of Asians, Hispanics, and women who are altering the appearance of the American office and changing the face of the American consumer. But even as I'm speaking, the numbers are already swelling and my material is out of date.

Percentages are ever-changing, but the philosophy of good business remains constant. That philosophy is this: Every individual in the marketplace, both the customer and the worker, deserves to be valued and respected, regardless of race, gender, age, religion, or socioeconomic status. Any business that tries to operate from a position of prejudice will learn quickly that, when it comes to employee and/or customer relations, bias doesn't pay.

The good news is that many companies are working hard to deal with the challenge of cultural diversity. Those that are especially effective target these six areas for intensive effort and attention.

- They address the attitudes of their workers, sponsoring educational workshops that highlight different cultures and their unique contributions. In this way, workers can learn to appreciate differences while recognizing their similarities.

- They emphasize good communication skills and encourage managers to affirm workers, giving value to their individual skills and accomplishments. Racial slurs are not tolerated.

- They provide career opportunities equally to all qualified candidates within the company.

- They address language barriers that may exist among workers.

- ✿ They enlist the help of mentors, role models, in developing the strength and integrity of their work force.

- ✿ They are alert and responsive to the ever-changing needs of their workplace and the marketplace and are willing to increase training opportunities.

In 1964, when the first black workers came through the doors of Corporate America carrying briefcases for the first time instead of mops and pails, wearing pin stripes instead of aprons and overalls, the companies that hired us didn't have any guidelines like these. And we who came to work for them had no guides.

That first generation of workers who integrated the office became pioneers, trailblazers. At times reluctant, often uncertain and fearful, we stepped warily, cautiously. We groped along, grabbing onto whatever ledge would hold us, pulling ourselves up, and smiling our thanks whenever a hand reached out to help us.

Things are better now for many of us. These days, most of Corporate America is integrated. Women, African Americans, Asian Americans, and Hispanics are a common sight in the company corridors. Still, it isn't far-fetched to find a "Lucy" in the lunchroom—a person who just doesn't understand that it's *not* okay for any segment of American society to be the denied dignity because of the shade of their skin.

And that's what a discussion of cultural diversity is all about. It's about helping people recognize simple human dignity in one another. It's about helping people accept the truth that different isn't inferior. It's about establishing relationships based on the similarities among us, while appreciating the differences that make each race, each ethnic group, unique and interesting.

Seminars and workshops, of course, can't solve every race-related problem in the workplace. Often, the best they can do is expose the need for understanding and respect while encouraging changes in attitudes. But the deepest, most significant changes occur when, one on one, individuals of different races make an effort to get acquainted with each other. When they try to understand each other and treat each other with respect. When the reasons for change are not solely for the purpose of business gains, even though that may be the motivation at the start.

For Lucy and me, our relationship grew slowly, never quite reaching the full bloom of friendship. I can't help but wonder if things might have been different between us if we'd ever crossed over into each other's social life after working hours. Maybe we'd be friends today if, say, one of us had had a Tupperware party and invited the other.

Who knows? The smallest gesture can be a beginning.

CHAPTER 7

FIGHT, FLIGHT, OR FINESSE

The early years of forced integration and mandatory hiring quotas were frustrating times for many employees of color. For me, it was a bittersweet dilemma.

I knew I was qualified for the job I held. I knew that if a dozen candidates had been interviewed, candidates of any color, I would have been as deserving as any, perhaps more. And daily I worked hard to prove that to my employer, the parts manager, Mr. Harris (not his real name), that, like him, I'd earned my position. But I was often reminded that, in his eyes, we were nothing at all alike.

I'll never forget one particular experience that proved just how different he perceived us to be.

Grannie called me at work one day, just before noon, telling me my son Little George was ill with a high fever. "The school nurse sent him home, Thelma, and said he ought to see a doctor today," she said. "He's a pretty sick little boy."

The common dilemma of the working mother, I thought, as I began trying to figure out how I could work until closing time, five o'clock, *and* get Little George to the doctor's office before it closed at five. I couldn't. I'd have to leave a little early. I knocked on Mr. Harris's door.

"Sir," I said, "My son is sick and I need to take him to the doctor."

Mr. Harris frowned.

"If I leave fifteen minutes early this afternoon I can get him in before the doctor closes for the day," I said. "Of course, I'll work through my afternoon break to make up for it."

Mr. Harris shook his head.

"No, Thelma."

No? Did he say no?

I couldn't believe what I'd heard.

"And I don't like you asking for favors," he added.

Favors? I thought, *what favors?* A bolt of hot anger surged through me. "I'm asking for what's mine," I said, holding my temper in a tight rein. "Those fifteen minutes are mine, and I need to use them to get my son to the doctor. And furthermore, I'm taking them, with or without your approval. In fact," I said, "I think I'll leave right now."

I walked out of his office, covered my typewriter, and left the building.

At home, I fumed and stomped.

"How dare he?" I said, as I bundled Little George into the car.

"How dare he?" I said, as I drove to the doctor's office.

That was on Wednesday. For the next three days I seethed with anger and refused to return to work. I called the plant manager—I thought I ought to explain my actions to someone—and when he heard what had happened, he apologized for Mr. Harris's behavior.

"That's not good enough," I said, still angry and reluctant to return to the office.

"I'm sure he's sorry, Thelma," the plant manager said, hoping to smooth things over. "Please come on back."

The following Monday, I drove back to the plant. Mr. Harris was waiting for me with an apology, of sorts.

"I am truly sorry, Thelma," Mr. Harris said. "But you have to understand, I thought this was just the beginning—you know, you'd be asking for time off all the time. I know how you people are, always asking for favors and taking advantage... Well, I just didn't want to let that get started."

The anger that had burned down to hot coals over five days flared up again, hotter than before.

"*You people?*" I bellowed. "Did you say *you people?* I don't believe this... " I was nearly stuttering now with fury. "Do you think we're really all that different, you and me? Do you think we don't love our children as much as you love yours? Mr. Harris, I love my son just like you love yours, and when he needs me I'll be there, just like you'll be there when your son needs you. If that means leaving early to take him to the doctor, then that's what I'll do, just like you would. And it won't be taking advantage, or asking for favors. I'll pull my weight around here, just like I always have. So don't you ever worry about me expecting anything that isn't already mine!"

Panting, I left his office and sat down heavily at my desk. I seethed as I typed, pounding the keys and throwing the carriage ferociously.

The anger I felt toward Mr. Harris did not dissipate quickly. For days, maybe weeks, I felt myself grow hot every time I thought about that confrontation. And worse, I felt a huge amount of stress that I hadn't ever known before, and I knew that most of it stemmed from uncertainty. What would happen when I faced a similar situation in the future? And there would be similar situations—I was a mother with children, and I would, at times, be needed at home during office hours.

Would Mr. Harris be difficult every time I needed special consideration? Would I be forced to fight for any small adjustment that might be needed to accommodate my personal life? If I challenged him, would I be forced to quit? Would he fire me?

I worked for Mr. Harris for four more years after that first disagreement. We were wary of each other and careful to try to maintain an uneasy peace. In time, I began to realize that, while race was a factor with Mr. Harris, our personality differences were also something to be considered. We were destined to collide, regardless of our skin color.

Now, thirty years later, I'm a little smarter about how personalities interact in the workplace. I know a little more about collision prevention, and I know that my reaction to Mr. Harris was all wrong. My response was an instinctive one, not an educated one. Nor was it a constructive one. My animal instincts, which direct us to fight or take flight, took over, and I had flown out of the office in fury. When I returned a few days later, I had followed my instincts again, only this time, I had chosen to fight. Now I know that there are better, more constructive approaches to conflict with a manager or boss. Today, I know I'd do things differently. Much differently.

Today, I would be sure I was *prepared* before I approached my manager about a sudden, unexpected change in the work routine.

Preparation is essential if an employee is going to be able to deal successfully with a difficult situation involving the boss. And that preparation means the employee has worked hard to accomplish these three prerequisites:

- Know the boss's personality type
- Document your work record
- Communicate regularly and candidly with your boss

Typically, four types of bosses inhabit the workplace. An astute employee needs only a few days of observation, noting the manager's communication style, to be able to identify whether the boss is: a) a controller, b) a supporter, c) a thinker, or d) an entertainer.

Knowing your boss's personality type will help you plan your approach when you must confront him or her with a situation that could erupt in conflict.

If your boss is like Mr. Harris, you're walking into the domain of a controller. True to his personality, he is *task-oriented*. Anything that threatens the completion of the task is going to cause him discomfort, and he will probably take it out on you. Often, this kind of boss seems arrogant, perhaps even rude. He may yell and scream and issue unreasonable edicts because his focus is on the job, not the person performing it. He may resort to intimidation tactics to control the office and the personnel, and he would rather say no than yes to any request that hasn't already been addressed in the company policy handbook.

And this is the person you have to approach about an unscheduled absence? If just thinking about it makes you reach for the Maalox bottle, take heart. It can be done, and you can do it. You're prepared, remember? Well, you're one-third of the way there. Because being prepared for difficult encounters in the office includes two more steps.

The second step of preparation requires careful, close documentation of all your work. You know what you've accomplished, how you've accomplished it; you know the mistakes you've made and how you've corrected them; you know how you've solved problems and what you have learned. You have a work schedule and you can show proof (documentation) that you have met that schedule. Your work habits are documented, your goals and objectives are defined, and you can walk into any boss's office with proof of your value to the company. You can—*if* your preparation didn't stop there; *if*, in your preparation, you also established methods of communicating with your boss on a regular schedule and in candid terms.

Quarterly or monthly meetings may be sufficient to keep the boss apprised of important matters in the office. During these meetings, an employee can stimulate communication by asking a few questions, such as:

- How do you see me relating to others in this department?

- How can I streamline or eliminate unnecessary tasks?

- What improvements would you suggest?

- In what areas am I doing well?

- What else can I do to improve the productivity of this office, department, company?

A meeting with the boss does more than answer these specific questions. It gives you an opportunity to peek inside the boss's head and figure out his needs and his style. Does he want small talk? Does he want to see charts and graphs? Does he prefer to communicate in memos or e-mail?

Maybe you've asked your boss for meetings of this sort. Maybe he's answered with a curt, "I'll let you know if you're not doing a good job." Don't worry. There's a lot of information in that answer. You're working for someone who doesn't want to spend time in meetings. Expect sparse praise for a job well done. If you ever make a major mistake, he'll aim his biggest guns at you, so be armed with a few Scud missiles of your own—your documented work record.

Documentation! It is essential in the workplace.

Now you're thoroughly prepared to face any kind of manager or boss with any kind of reasonable request. You just have to customize your communication style to suit your boss's. For a Mr. Harris, a control freak who is aloof and private, you must be businesslike. Don't try to make small talk with this boss. And don't try to tell him what to do.

In an encounter with a controlling boss, *asking,* not telling, is extremely important. He is able to maintain his sense of control as long as you are *asking* (although the person who asks the last question most often holds control of the conversation).

Show your documentation—you've been doing your work well, you're not behind on any projects. Show your plan for making up whatever time you are taking off. And make sure he *sees* your documentation—people are less likely to be difficult when they see that you have the facts.

It's possible that, like Mr. Harris, your manager may reject your request, even though it is a reasonable one. Instead of stomping out of the office in anger, like I did, and sulking, and giving up three days' pay, you do have other options.

"Mr. Harris," I might have said, "I've tried to be reasonable with you, and now you leave me no choice but to speak to your superior. Would you like to come with me? Perhaps a third party could help us mediate this standoff. I will, of course, document this encounter, in case there should be any questions about it later."

Now that I'm thirty years older, I would conduct myself in a more professional way and expect a better outcome if I had to face conflict with a controlling boss.

Not all managers are like Mr. Harris (thank God!). Some are more like the type I call "Helpful Honey." Their greatest fear in life is injuring someone's feelings. No task orientation in this boss—she's relationship-oriented, and while she may be helpful, friendly, warm, and considerate of her staff, she is also often vague about her expectations in the workplace.

The "Helpful Honey" knows what must be done and what is required of each employee, but her need to be loved often interferes with her ability to deal with her staff on a professional level. She may listen to an employee's legitimate request to leave early, and she may want to say yes (she wants you to love her), but sometimes it's not easy. If *her* boss has expressed concern about recent absenteeism in the department, she will feel extra pressure. She will probably grant your request anyway, but she'll feel angry with herself afterward, and she will hold a grudge against the worker who's caused such conflicted emotions.

"Honeys" are usually master manipulators and guilt-slingers. A typical "Honey" comment may sound something like, "You go ahead, we'll manage, but this will put an awful strain on the department... no, no, you go on... "

If you're dealing with a "Honey" of a boss, you'll need to be firm in your presentation. Show her your documentation. Give her a specific time when she can expect the work on her desk. Show concern for her—she's under a boss's eye too—and make sure she understands that you will carry your weight and you're not expecting her to do your work.

"Helpful Honey" wants and needs to be liked, but she also needs reassurance. Give her what she needs and she is likely to give you what you need without trying to inflict guilt.

The boss I call "Data Chip" is a thinker and an analyzer. These people need guarantees, not reassurances. They don't care about being liked *or* being in control. They care about the bottom line. And they may be the hardest to communicate with.

"Chips" are often systems-oriented. If all your efforts to schedule a monthly or quarterly meeting have failed, try reaching "Chip" via E-mail.

When presented with an unexpected request, "Chip" will probably give a precise, unemotional "No." He's a lot like his computer—anything that isn't already in the program is considered a glitch and should be deleted, and that includes your unexpected knock on his office door.

When you have to ask for special consideration that will affect the usual office routine, go in with your documentation in hand. Show "Chip" what needs to be done, how you've organized to get it done, and present him with proof that you've been successful in the past. Show him your prioritized tasks, and let your past record of diligence reassure him that your departure from normal routine will have no negative impact on the bottom line.

"Chip" may force you to go over his head, as I should have done with the controlling Mr. Harris. If this happens, the procedure is the same: invite him to come along, bring documentation, remain professional at all times.

No one is easier to work for than the boss with the entertainer's persona. These people like nothing better than to be applauded. They thrive on being noticed and praised and are usually easily approached and readily convinced of the need to work with you in special circumstances. You can probably walk into their offices and tell them what you need without any fear that they'll say no.

But it is important to remember that, because they want to look good and be praised, they will want you to reassure them that work will not be disrupted in any measurable way. If you suddenly need to leave early or come in late or take off Thursday afternoon, reassure "Mr. Saturday Night" that this won't hurt the department's shiny image. Productivity will not suffer. The "entertainer" will appreciate it if you demonstrate protectiveness toward his reputation and the department that he heads. He's the one credited, or blamed, for the performance of the team. And like all performers, he prefers a good review to a bad one.

Any boss, of any personality type, will have his or her own set of prejudices—racial, socioeconomic, religious, or any other. And like Mr. Harris, they may take these prejudices with them to the office. While we do have some laws that protect workers from abusive treatment, some employees still encounter rude, prejudiced bosses who enjoy slinging slurs and making racial comments. Some may even try to penalize employees for skin color or the shape of their eyes.

My best advice for the employee who feels as though she is being abused or treated unfairly is to document your work. Be able to show proof of your accomplishments and your work habits. Document every abusive encounter with the boss, letting him or her know that you are recording the incidents. And be ready to respond in the most professional manner possible.

Refuse to allow the discussion to slide onto a personal level. Emphasize your job performance and show proof of your contribution to the goals and objectives of the department and the company as a whole. This will be your strongest ally if the conflict becomes large enough to need the help of a mediator.

I've worked for all kinds of managers—the Mr. Harrises who dominate the office with their dictatorial style and their obsessive need to be in control; the "Helpful Honeys" who have to be loved and who need constant reassurance that the job will get done and everyone will be happy; the "Data Chip" who prefers his computer to human beings and is in need of guarantees that the bottom line is not under threat; and the "entertainer" whose greatest need is to look good at all times, at all costs. Each type has unique strengths and weaknesses. Each type brings a valuable contribution to the workplace.

I've learned that getting along with anyone, of any personality type, regardless of individual prejudices or petty attitudes, requires effort and savvy planning.

The "fight or flight" concept works well for creatures roaming the wilds. They're well suited for roaring, retaliating, and racing for the safety of a tall tree or the cover of a cave. But in the corporate jungle, where few trees and even fewer caves are found, it can be disastrous. Here, safety more often depends on ignoring our instincts and remembering this: Survival is not only a matter of fitness, it is also a matter of finesse.

CHAPTER 8

WHEN CRISIS STRIKES
THE HEART

A crisis can come in almost any kind of package.

I've learned that unwrapping it, handling it, exposing it to other eyes helps me understand it and know what to do with it. Most of my life, I depended on Grannie's eyes and hands. When suddenly Grannie was stilled and silenced by a series of strokes, I found myself bereft, almost helpless, when circumstances thrust me into an unfamiliar emergency.

After several years with J.D. Enterprises, a complicated pregnancy forced me to resign and accept the doctor's command to spend the next seven months in bed. That was not the emergency, although it was a difficult, exasperating time for me.

When our daughter Lesa was born in May 1969, our family celebrated and life resumed a sort of normalcy, although I was unable to return to my old job at J.D. Enterprises. Maternity leave was an idea that awaited women of the future. If I wanted to go back to J.D. Enterprises, I'd have to reapply and accept whatever opening matched my skills and experience. My old job was not available. But I didn't view that as a crisis.

I had grown tired of typing parts numbers on forms long before the doctor told me I'd have to quit working. In fact, I'd prayed, "Lord, get me out of this job!" I'd never expected the answer He sent, but neither did I grieve over having to say goodbye to Mr. Harris. No emergency there.

I decided to stay home for a few months, working part-time and enjoying my new daughter. Grannie was growing frail, but she was able to care for the baby a few hours a day, so I accepted temporary jobs. My plan was that as soon as Lesa was able to go to nursery school, I would accept a full-time position in the corporate world. George's business was stable. Part-time income would be sufficient for a while. Again, still no crisis.

The plan unraveled quickly. Only a few short months after I began working part-time, Grannie's health began to decline rapidly. As her movements became slower and more painful, I could see that caring for Lesa was too much for her. She argued with me when I told her I had decided to quit working; she insisted I wasn't needed at home. But I knew, for both Lesa's and Grannie's sake, I could no longer leave them alone.

Grannie had always looked forward to the afternoons when the older children, Vikki and Little George, came home after school, but these days she was too exhausted to enjoy them. Instead of lingering over supper with the family, she retired to her room early, spending more and more time in bed. Then one day, she was unable to get up. A final stroke rendered her partially paralyzed and unable to speak.

I had known this day would come eventually. Grannie was my *great*-grandmother, and she had been an old woman, even when I was a little girl. But even in her frailty, I had leaned on her and depended on her wisdom. Now, I would have to be the strong one and let her do the leaning. It was not a natural posture for me, but I would do what I had to for Grannie. This did not constitute an emergency. That would come later, after several months of being alone and lonely in a house all day, caring for three small children and a silent, bedridden elderly woman.

The crisis that was my undoing was one of the heart and the spirit. And, now with the vantage of hindsight and a bit more knowledge of life and human nature, I know that it is a crisis common to most people. We label it by different names, sometimes calling it a crisis of self-esteem, but when it hits the spirit of a man or woman, it is nothing less than disastrous.

A crisis of self-esteem cuts deep into the personality, slicing at every nerve that would try to tell you that you are valuable, worthwhile, and precious. It jabs and taunts with messages that say, "You'll never be anything. You'll never do anything significant. You're as necessary as dryer lint, and just about as attractive." A spirit that has endured these attacks is left limp and hurting and willing to believe it really is useless and ugly.

I know. I began to believe these things about myself, and I figured everyone who knew me believed them too. Except George, but his reassurances came all too seldom. His business demands were extreme, and when he was home, the distractions of routine family life were many. We began to miss the extra income I had been able to earn throughout our marriage, and I missed that feeling of satisfaction that comes from being able to contribute in tangible, measurable ways—like dollars for children's shoes and car repairs and household maintenance.

And I missed Grannie's voice. I had never realized how much I had relied on her sound wisdom, her loving affirmation, and her strong encouragement. Now silent and partially paralyzed, she could neither speak to me nor hold me in her arms and rock me until the feelings of futility and emptiness passed.

And so crisis struck.

Like a hurricane, blowing down every structure in its wide path, the storm of insecurity that hit me demolished me from the inside out, destroying all my self-confidence.

I awakened each morning feeling empty, without purpose. I trudged through the day's routine, anxious to get it all over with so I could go to sleep again. Sleep was a respite, it gave me small moments of escape, if only between Lesa's feedings and hourly checks on Grannie. And the next day it all began again, exactly as the day before, except that the guilt I felt seemed to multiply overnight.

I've got to get out of here, I thought often. If I could just go back to work...

And then a shovelful of guilt would splatter in my face.

A *good* mother wouldn't be so anxious to leave her baby and go back to an office, I thought. A *good* mother would enjoy being home, and a *good* daughter wouldn't begrudge caring for the woman who had raised her.

It was a quick trip from guilt to self-hatred. And from

there, it took only one small step to hurl me into a deep depression.

At that time in my life, I believed that only work could cure my ills. I thought it was the only route to sanity. And because that route was blocked, I felt trapped.

I loved my children and my home, as well as dear Grannie, but the workplace was where I found my greatest sense of satisfaction. There my tasks could be completed and documented and achievement could be measured. Yes, I had faced conflict and prejudice and frustrating situations, but as I'd met each obstacle and overcome it (or, at least not laid down and died), I'd felt strength pump through my veins. I'd felt powerful, indomitable. I'd felt euphoric. At home, success was not so easily defined. Here, the greatest challenge in a day might be scrubbing brown crayon off the dining room wall. It just didn't offer the same surge.

At home and without help, I felt strained beyond my limits, and yet there was always more to do. And moments later, it would need to be done again. It all seemed so overwhelmingly futile, but there was nothing I could do to change it. For the first time in my life, I felt out of control. And isolated.

How small my world seemed. Too small. It consisted only of diaper pails, cooking utensils, restless children, and the dying elderly.

I was at my most desperate point of misery when neighbors encouraged me to get involved with the Hamilton Park Civic League.

George and I had been a part of this group of homeowners, six hundred in all, since we'd first moved into the neighborhood. I had attended meetings to discuss the needs of our community, but my involvement had been limited by my work schedule. Now my household demands were even more limiting, but I felt an urgency about getting to the league meetings. I found a sitter willing to care for both Lesa and Grannie and, for a few short hours once a week, I walked away from piles of children's toys and Grannie's silent presence.

I entered a room filled with people committed to one another and to the cause of improving their community. I entered a room where ideas were discussed, where debate occurred, where men and women put aside their individual concerns and focused on the larger issues that affected us all. And when I went home to the children and George and Grannie, I felt refreshed. I felt renewed.

When I reflect on that long-ago time, I am incredulous. It began with such frustration and futility, but it became the most challenging and productive phase of my life.

Within the Hamilton Park Civic League, I made new friends and reestablished relationships with old friends. Some, like Mrs. Willie B. Johnson, a longtime friend of Grannie's, seemed to sense my need for encouragement and affirmation. She became Grannie's voice in my ear, telling me the loving, supportive things I needed to hear.

An energetic woman, Mrs. Johnson was an activist who never tired of working for our community. I knew her strength and her vision. All my life I'd attended St. John Missionary Baptist Church, where she was a member, and I'd grown up with her children. Now, she was my neighbor and my mentor. No one was more pleased than she when I was elected president of the Hamilton Park Civic League. And no one was more supportive of my efforts at leadership.

"Little Thelma," she said, one day, "you need to make a few phone calls to the city council. We need to get a meeting to talk about a bond election."

I would always be "Little Thelma" to Mrs. Johnson, but to the Dallas City Council, I represented a strong and ever-growing block of voters—the homeowners in Hamilton Park. We were vocal, well-organized, and determined. With people like Willie B. Johnson to motivate and steer us, we campaigned together, urging City Hall to take notice of the needs of our neighborhood.

Hamilton Park was built on a flood plain. We had no drainage. Whenever it rained, our streets became rivers and our one small park a bog. Only one street served as an entrance into our neighborhood, so if it was blocked or flooded, no one could get in or out of Hamilton Park. The agenda for the civic league included correcting these problems, in addition to getting street lights, gaining representation on the Richardson district school board, and improving the park for our children.

In time, all our goals were achieved. I was never more proud and gratified than on the day the Hamilton Park Civic League dedicated its refurbished neighborhood park with its new swimming pool and playground equipment and announced its new name: The Willie B. Johnson Recreation Center.

Hamilton Park was, from its beginning, a unique corner in the northeast quadrant of Dallas. In the mid- to late sixties, it was like a small enclave, almost, in a city warring with the concept of desegregation. It fought its battles in the voting booth and in the city council chambers and then retreated to its quiet streets to regroup and regain strength and perspective. I will always be grateful for the privilege of having lived there and learned the lessons it had to share.

I learned the power of good politics and the strength of unity. But in addition to lessons of community and cooperation, I learned something else. Something perhaps equally important, equally constructive. I discovered the route back to healthy self-esteem.

Of all the workshops and seminars I teach throughout the year, the ones dealing with self-esteem are the most requested. These also trigger the most audience response.

Everyone, at some time, experiences feelings of worthlessness. We all know how it feels to wake up and wonder if there is any reason to get out of bed today. And we've all asked ourselves, whether consciously or unconsciously, what possible good am I contributing by being alive? And we've answered ourselves with a depressing, None.

For some people, questions like these have accompanied them all their lives. They've never been far from the sound of that cruel voice that tells them they're worthless, unlovely, and unnecessary to the human race. For others, the messages began intruding later, in response to a sudden, deep loss or an unexpected, unpleasant change in life. For all of us, the pain is the same: harsh and unrelenting. But, thankfully, a remedy does exist.

It is a simple remedy, really, consisting of only eight ingredients, and it can be administered in the home or in the office. Regardless of who you are or where you are, the results will be the same. You may be a mother at home with small children tugging on your legs, or a cashier ringing sales in a grocery store, or an executive in a penthouse office discussing the shareholders' profits. It doesn't matter. Whoever you are and whatever your career or station in life, this remedy will work for you. It will soothe and revive a damaged spirit and will restore health to anyone suffering from injured self-esteem.

❦ Find yourself a cheerleader.

Grannie was the first to cheer for me. From earliest childhood, I knew she believed in me. I was fortunate to have others join Grannie until I had an entire community—including church, school, and neighborhood—as my own personal squad. They stood on the sidelines, encouraging me, shouting affirmation and support. My crisis of self-esteem occurred when I no longer heard the voices of support. The crisis began to abate when Willie B. Johnson took up my cause and began to cheer for me.

We all need to be reminded that we are valuable, that we are valued. If you are in a crisis period right now without the voice of a cheerleader, think about the person who most recently encouraged you. Can you call that person and thank them for the words they spoke that awakened hope in you? Make the call or write a note of thanks and let them know how important their encouragement is. Ask for more! And offer them support as well. Try to schedule time with the people who are your cheerleaders. Listen to them, believe them. Write down the words of encouragement they've said to you— use note cards and carry them with you for a while. Remind yourself that someone you respect also respects you and believes in your value.

❦ Find a mentor.

The quest for healthy self-esteem leads not only to the people who will affirm us and compliment us, it also leads us to those who will tell us the hard things we need to hear. It leads us to mentors, the men and women who know us and respect us enough to confront us when we're wrong, to direct us back onto the right road when we've lost our way. These people will tell us the truth about ourselves, even if it is painful.

My husband's aunt, Doretha, has been an important mentor in my life. Through the years, she has scolded me, confronted me, advised me, and directed me, and I have listened because I respect her. Her life is a testament to her wisdom and her integrity.

Grannie and Mrs. Johnson, while they were encouragers, were also very willing to confront me when necessary. Their advice and instructions guided me through many situations. Both of these wise women knew that it was important that I have a sense of personal significance, but they knew it is equally important that I listen to the painful, sometimes unpleasant and difficult truths about myself, my job, my relationships.

The message that a mentor sends is this: Because you are valuable to me, because I love and respect you, I must tell you the truth as I see it.

What a powerful message. It is essential to the building of healthy self-esteem.

🐝 Focus on an issue larger than yourself.

Wherever we are, in the home or in the corporate environment, we need to be reminded of the larger world beyond.

My involvement in the Hamilton Park Civic League allowed me to do this. It allowed me, for a few hours every week, to be a part of something that transcended the mundane. It allowed me to enlarge my view of life and make room for thoughts and visions that encompassed territory outside the walls of my small house, beyond the personalities of the members of my family.

All of us need a place where we are challenged to think beyond the limits of our own zip code. For most of us, such a place is as near as our local church. For others, it may be a youth sports league, or a local parent-teacher association, or an inner-city soup kitchen. Anyplace that encourages us to be part of an effort that is working toward a common good is a healthy place to be, if only for a few hours a week. It affords us a chance to rid our thoughts of trivia and concentrate on things of substance.

Spending time in endeavors that address the larger issues of life has a way of altering our perspective. It can change the way we see ourselves and our lives. It can influence our attitude, enabling us to replace self-absorption with selflessness, self-pity with gratitude.

People with healthy self-esteem have learned to see that the tiny space they inhabit, while important, is not the only space. It is but a small speck on the canvas of a much larger picture.

🐦 Set reasonable, attainable goals for yourself.

One of the reasons I experienced such a crisis of self-esteem stemmed from the fact that, for the first time in my life, I had no goals to challenge me. Many women who have chosen to stay home with young children have admitted that this is a problem for them. But it is not unique to women at home. Men and women, in every kind of work setting, will find themselves unfulfilled and unsatisfied if they do not learn to set realistic goals, both long-term and short-term.

We all need to feel some sense of accomplishment. Whether we are aware of it or not, we are constantly evaluating ourselves, comparing ourselves—to people and to standards people set. If we set our own goals, making them realistic and attainable, our self-evaluation will be a positive experience. It will give us encouragement and feelings of satisfaction.

In the office, a long-term goal might be the achieving of a managerial position. A short-term goal might be reaching the week's sales quota.

A professional woman once told me that one of the most satisfying times in her life was while she was a young, stay-at-home mother. When her children were small, she had begun trying to write for publication. She could do it at home, a few hours a day, while the children slept or played. She set a reasonable goal for herself, given the likelihood of frequent interruption, and determined to write and sell one article per month. It wasn't a huge goal, but it was manageable. At the end of the year, with a dozen magazine articles in print, she could hardly contain the satisfaction she felt. I wasn't surprised to learn that she later fulfilled her long-term goal—that of writing a book.

Short and long-term goals, reasonable and attainable, give pleasure, challenge, and purpose to any job, in any setting. And they can do a lot to lift a plunging sense of self-esteem.

🐾 Continue learning.

Knowledge is power, it has been said. And gaining new knowledge is a powerful tool for building self-esteem.

I have felt the wonder of learning, of facing a problem with a new set of solutions, and it is a heady feeling. How wonderful it is to be able to compute life's events, to make good decisions, and to contribute to my community, because I am educated and informed and trained.

Learning enlarges your world and enhances your personality. Learning increases your sense of value to the world. Learning gives you a great sense of well-being. Learning builds self-esteem.

Whether you enroll in continuing education at a high school or a community college, whether you use audio or visual tools as study guides, knowledge is accessible. Knowledge is available.

Today, we accept no alibis for being deficient.

🐾 Find ways to give to others without expecting anything in return.

It is something of a paradox, but when we are most emptied of self-interest, we are most fulfilled.

Ask anyone who has learned the lessons of giving just for the sake of giving. They will tell you that it is truly better to give than to receive. They will tell you that the search for healthy self-esteem will end in disappointment if, at some point, it does not shift its focus and begin seeking ways to satisfy the needs of others.

We can give without demand for a reward through volunteerism, through church ministries, through neighborhood and community organizations. On a more personal level, we can give our time, our skills, our friendship, to a neighbor or a co-worker without requiring anything in return.

When we give unselfishly, without any thought of being praised or rewarded, what we gain far outweighs what we have contributed. A sweet sense of satisfaction fills us, for by giving away, we have somehow been nourished.

🐝 Forgive others and yourself.

You can't have a healthy sense of self-esteem if you are harboring hard feelings toward others or toward yourself. If you haven't done it before, *now* is the time to forgive.

If you're struggling with the idea of "forgive and forget," and you'd really like to, but the "forgetting" part is too hard, let me suggest a different approach. Try thinking of forgiveness as an ongoing event. It is seldom accomplished by a one-time statement of "I forgive you." It is something you have to do every time that hurtful experience comes to mind. Today, you make a decision to forgive again, because today the memory causes pain again. And today, you choose to release your grip on those hard and angry feelings you hold against the one who hurt you.

You may have to look in the mirror and say to yourself, "I forgive you, and I'm not going to keep on punishing you for something stupid and hurtful you did ten years ago."

Forgiveness is a process, and it is usually a lifetime project. The goal is to *get over it!*

I'm a recovering perfectionist. Every day I remind myself that perfectionists are psychotic, neurotic individuals trying in vain to live up to their own and others' standards—standards that no human being can reach. Every day I have to tell myself to "get over it" when I don't live up to those standards. I tell myself they are too high—they can never be achieved. Still, undeterred, every day I try and fail and, every day I have to tell myself it's okay. It's okay, Thelma, I remind myself. You aren't perfect, now don't punish yourself for it!

I realize that some hurts are so deep and some wounds so serious that a simple "Get over it!" is inadequate. To those of you who are struggling with injuries that need special tending, let me encourage you to seek help. See a counselor who will let you talk about the pain and then guide you toward recovery.

Healthy self-esteem requires that you leave the inequities of the past behind you. That can't be done if you're dragging them along with you and pulling them out for morbid display. Maybe today would be a good day to release them.

❧ Exercise deep faith in God.

From childhood, I believed that God loved me and was concerned about my life. Over time, I have experienced His power at work in many circumstances. I've learned that His strength is there for me when I am weak. He has assigned value to my life, so who am I to try to convince Him that I am worthless?

A crisis of self-esteem can strike anyone, regardless of how confident we may appear on the outside. None of us are immune. And it can strike at anytime.

I recently conducted a series of seminars for a company in an East Coast city. At the close of the conference I felt very satisfied. The audience response was enthusiastic, the company executives who had invited me offered praise and invited me back for the next year, and when I left for home, my self-esteem was at an all-time high. A few days later, after I read a six-page letter full of criticism from a man who'd been in the audience, my sense of self-worth belonged in a bowl you could flush with a chrome handle.

The letter attacked me on both a personal and professional level, citing my material, my delivery, and my appearance. After the shock of it subsided, anger and hurt settled in. And then self-doubt followed quickly, leaving me with thoughts like, Maybe he's right, Thelma, maybe you really are worthless.

It was a dangerous mind game, this I knew. And I didn't dare allow myself to play it for very long. I decided it was a good time to review the material I teach in my self-esteem workshops. It was a good time for the teacher to become the student.

I pulled out my notes, all the handouts and the charts, and I looked over the eight ingredients that I believe are essential for healthy self-esteem. And then I picked up the phone and made a call to my daughter Vikki.

Vikki is one of my most enthusiastic cheerleaders, so I talked with her about the letter and the feelings it had prompted. I listened as she reminded me, "Mom, five hundred people in that seminar shook your hand and thanked you for the great information. You can't count all the words of praise and appreciation you heard that day. Why are you obsessing on the one person who criticized you?"

Why, indeed, I thought. And then I called Hattie Hill-Storks, a fellow speaker and seminar leader who I consider a mentor as well as a friend. Together we talked about the critical remarks I'd received, and we evaluated my material. Was there need for change? Where could I improve?

For the next few days, I concentrated on the eight ingredients needed for healthy self-esteem. I examined them all. And I determined to practice them all, testing them for truth and effectiveness. And I proved to myself, again, that feeling lousy about myself doesn't have to be a permanent condition. That it is possible to find relief.

I proved to myself that self-esteem is not only a matter of the heart and the spirit, it is a matter of the mind and the body. By that I mean that what we *feel* can be changed by what we *think* and *do*.

We can wallow in emotional misery, or we can decide to get up and do something about our feelings. For some, it may be the hardest work they'll ever do, but in the end they'll discover, as I did, that work is preferable to wallowing, any day.

CHAPTER 9

SO YOU THINK YOU'RE
A LEADER

Grannie died the summer of 1972. She had been silent and still, dependent upon continual care for the most intimate of needs for more than two years, but her passing was the greatest wrenching I have ever known. Without her presence, the house in Hamilton Park felt like an empty cavern to me. Loneliness seemed to vibrate in every room, and all I wanted to do was flee from it.

After enrolling Lesa in preschool that fall, I picked up my skirts and ran to the closest job recruiter's office. A few weeks later, I accepted a full-time position as a proof operator with a large Dallas bank, balancing and proving large accounts. Thus ended my three-year exile from corporate America.

The business of banking was a natural for me. I learned quickly and advanced through the training levels easily. In 1974, I joined the staff of another fine bank, and a year later I began taking classes at the American Institute of Banking. The following year, I was teaching them. A few short months later, my employer promoted me to supervisor of bookkeeping and customer services.

It was a comparatively quick climb from entry level clerk to supervisor, and I felt proud that I had accomplished so much in so little time. I was determined to be worthy of the responsibility entrusted to me. I could think of no reason why I shouldn't have the best department in the bank.

In the beginning all went well. The employees in my department did their jobs, the bank officers were pleased, the department functioned the way it should, and I thought,

Thelma, you're doing a fine job. Nobody could do it better.

You're a natural-born leader, I thought, patting myself on the back.

My thoughts were much less congratulatory after I took a look at my department's turnover rate. It was one of the highest in the company.

Why were the people under me quitting or asking for departmental transfers so frequently? What was wrong in my corner of the bank?

In the process of firing a difficult, inept employee, I learned some painful realities about my leadership style. During her exit interview, the fired employee said I was stingy with praise, rigid with orders, and quick to find fault with the people under me.

"Thelma never tells us when we do well," she said. "But if we make a mistake, she's all over us like a tent."

I listened to the woman's comments and, like most people who are being criticized, I felt angry at first.

How dare this woman say these things about me? I thought. Sure, I run a tight ship, but this is a bank. You can't afford to be sloppy in this business.

When the anger subsided, I began to think more rationally about the criticisms leveled at me. And I began to scrutinize my leadership style. I looked back at the way I had handled some of the personnel situations in my department, and I had to confess, I hadn't done a very good job.

Take, for instance, the matter of the woman who refused to bathe. I'd really fumbled on that one. She was a recent immigrant from another country, and she had not yet adapted to our American hygiene practices. For weeks, the people in my department had come to me with complaints about the stench in the office. When I did nothing, they decided to act. They began leaving little hints on her desk, anonymously, of course—cans of deodorant, bars of soap, shampoo, cheap perfume. But nothing helped. The woman continued to come to work smelling terrible, and I continued to do nothing.

Finally, struggling with the delicacy of the matter, I phoned the woman's sister, who was a familiar bank customer. We agreed that she would speak to her sister for me. It was a classic hand-off—and on this play too, I fumbled miserably.

In the end, I theorized that only the direct approach would work. I called the employee into my office, and in complete privacy, I said, "You are not bathing. In this country, people bathe frequently and use deodorant. I realize things are different in the culture you came from, but this is America, and we consider body odor offensive. In an office like this, where we work closely, it is essential that you practice good personal hygiene."

I gave her a list of products to use and told her that she had to cooperate in this matter for the sake of office morale.

The problem was solved immediately. To my surprise, the employee seemed grateful for my help. After that conversation, she sought my advice on other aspects of assimilation into American culture.

Good job, Thelma, I told myself.

But the solving of one problem meant only that more awaited me. I still had much to learn about leadership.

Oh, I knew something about being a "boss," but that wasn't at all the same as being a good leader.

I was very good at telling people what to do and how to do it, but I wasn't very good at motivating them to excellence. I wasn't successful at pulling out the best in people and imparting to them the confidence it takes to solve problems creatively. My record of grooming employees for advancement was poor. And the turnover figures continued to indicate that my employees thought of my department not as an office but as a stalag to be escaped. I remember sitting at my desk, my head in my hands, and thinking, Now, what are you going to do, Thelma Wells?

The answer was simple: I was going to overhaul my leadership technique. I was going to learn how to be a creative, constructive leader.

It's been said that he who is taught only by himself has a fool for a teacher. The people I worked with made sure that didn't happen to me. They became my teachers, giving me valuable lessons about leadership that could never be learned from a lecture. The office, our entire department, became a classroom for me, and every day I found opportunities to experiment with a variety of techniques.

Sandra (not her real name) taught me about dealing with employees who gripe about other employees. Nobody could please Sandra. She complained constantly, coming to me with reports of co-workers who were making personal calls on company time, co-workers who spent too much time in the bathroom, co-workers who came back late from break. Every day she assaulted me with her stories of employees who weren't doing the job and employees who were wasting company time.

And every day I wanted to throttle her for her meddling, but every day I let her come in and inform on the other workers. She was an older employee with seniority, and she seemed to believe it was her duty to spy on everyone in the department. I didn't know how to stop it. I tried acting too busy to listen, but she persisted until I looked up from my work. I tried ignoring her, but she followed me down hallways, into the coffee lounge, sometimes into the rest room, always chattering about the misdeeds of her fellow workers.

One day I decided to try something new with Sandra. Instead of ignoring her when she stepped into my office to complain and inform, instead of groaning inwardly and wishing she would go away, I paid close attention to what she was saying, then I picked up pen and pad and jotted down a few quick notes.

"I'm listening, Sandra," I said. "This is very interesting, but of course you know that I can't take any action against an employee unless I have something in writing. As you can see, I'm noting that you've come in with a report, but you'll have to write down any office offenses you see, recording the name, date, and time of day you observed them."

Sandra looked startled.

"Starting today, Sandra, I want you to document every infraction you see. I can't be in the outer office every minute, and if these things are really going on, they should be documented," I told her. "I'm glad to have you out there watching, and I want you to make a chart for each employee, by name, and record everything you see."

Sandra blinked and started to speak. I interrupted her.

"If someone leaves early, write it down," I said. "And if you hear anyone making a personal call, make a note. Keep the chart for a month, and then we'll see what kind of action needs to be taken against the employees."

"Well, I don't know," Sandra said, backing toward the door, "I mean, I just wanted to let you know what's going on in the department, but I don't have time to be keeping a chart on everybody."

I shrugged. "Sandra, if you don't bring me documentation, there is nothing I can do."

Sandra huffed and frowned, tightening her clutch on her note pad. "I'm not going to keep a chart on my co-workers," she said firmly.

"Well, then, I guess you won't be bringing me complaints about them anymore," I answered.

Sandra turned around abruptly and walked back to her desk, plunging into a pile of papers.

That was the end of Sandra's meddling.

I wasn't a seasoned leader, but by experimenting, I learned an effective technique for handling office troublemakers. Since then, I've discovered that many successful office managers employ that same technique to deal with workers who complain about their co-workers. They assign them what is called "completed staff work," which is similar to the chart I told Sandra to make. This simple assignment places the burden of proof on the employee who may be complaining. It usually results in quieting the whiners. I could give a dozen other examples of leadership tactics I tried that did *not* work, all part of trial and error, but the important point is this: *good* leaders are made, not born. While some individuals may appear to have come into the world with certain personality traits we associate with leadership, *good* leaders know that there is a lot to learn about leading people, and they have applied themselves to the task of learning and improving their skills. They understand the role of a leader.

THE LEADER'S ROLE

Good leaders have essentially two obligations: They must perform their individual tasks, and they must ensure that those who work for them do their tasks as well, so that the goals of the company are achieved.

It looks simple. But as I found out, leading is anything but simple. However, having a sound philosophy for leadership does make it somewhat easier. I found that I became a better leader when I defined my role in two terms. First, as a coach, and second, as a guide.

✤ The leader as coach

We expect leaders, like coaches, to know something about the business that employs them. If they don't, we're in serious trouble. We expect them to be knowledgeable and somewhat experienced in the industry so that their decisions as leaders are intelligent and informed ones. After all, they are making decisions that affect those who work for (with) them. We want to trust their insight. We want to be able to work without concern that their behavior or decisions will put our jobs at risk. We need to know that they know what they are doing. This is true for anyone who aspires to be a leader, whether coaching on a gridiron or running a department in the corporate community.

Leaders are in a position of authority, and if leaders are to be followed, it is essential that they demonstrate skill and intelligence. That means coming to work prepared and equipped to do the job for which they were hired. The success of their team depends on it.

Good leaders, like good coaches, also understand that, while their position represents authority, they cannot achieve success unless they understand the principle of interdependence. They know that they are part of a team, and as such, they must depend upon and value the contribution of all the other personnel.

Listen to a postgame interview with the National Basketball Association's Paul Westphal, coach of the Phoenix Suns. In every conversation regarding his work, he acknowledges and praises the players, because he knows that without a team, he cannot coach. How foolish an NBA coach would appear if he claimed for himself all the credit for the success of the Phoenix Suns. Imagine the affront that would be to Patrick

Ewing and the other outstanding athletes who go out on the court and sweat and slam dunk to win games and bring home trophies. Think of Charles Barkley's reaction if his coach ignored his contribution and accepted all the accolades for the team's success.

Good leaders know that interdependence is the key to good teamwork. Each person is essential. They know that leadership is not solitary work, performed in isolation. It is a task undergirded by the energy and efforts of others. The leader who forgets or ignores this concept risks alienating his team and forfeiting all chances of success and achievement.

Good leaders, like good coaches, go to the office equipped with knowledge and expertise. They know their job, and they show up ready to do it well and with enthusiasm. They value the contribution of each team member, and they accept their responsibility as leaders to draw out of their employees the best possible job performance. They understand it is their job to *empower* their staff.

Empowering people means enabling them to do the job for which they were hired and to do it with excellence and with confidence. And like many important endeavors, empowering workers is an ongoing process, encompassing a multitude of large and small initiatives. Here are the ones that are both obvious and essential:

🐾 Empowering means identifying the unique strengths and special skills of each team member and then placing them in a position on which those skills can be used to optimum advantage.

🐾 Empowering means treating the members of your team with respect and fairness, regardless of race, religion, appearance, or physical challenge. This enables each person to work without the distractions of worry and distrust or fear of discrimination. Also, your example of fairness toward and respect for each individual lessens the risk of hostility and unhealthy relationships among team members.

❦ Empowering means communicating clearly and often with your team, making sure everyone understands departmental instructions, expectations, and company goals. Uncertainty in any setting can breed confusion and the unsettledness that comes from feeling out of control—complications a good leader will want to avoid. She will communicate with her employees to ensure that each person feels informed and comfortable with the company's expectations. This will involve occasional evaluations, which may include suggestions for improvement as well as praise. A good leader knows that healthy, open communication within a company usually results in increased productivity and improved morale, so she will make it a priority to be sure everyone understands what is expected of her, individually and as a part of the team.

❦ Empowering means helping your team unite in the pursuit of a common goal. Again, who does it better than coaches? They talk about winning the tournament and going on to the "final four." In the old days of baseball, before the strike, they talked about "winning it all!" Going to the World Series. Gather a handful of individuals and give them the vision of a big win—one that can only be accomplished if each one does his part, his *very best* part, and you have the spirit of an Olympic team. You have the mentality of winners. Office leaders can create that same kind of winning attitude by setting goals that can be achieved only if everyone applies their best efforts. The bond of cooperation that is forged in the pursuit of such a goal is in many ways as valuable to the company as any financial gain that might be achieved in the end.

❦ Empowering means making strategic plans for your team's success. Imagine a coach without a game plan. Imagine Vince Lombardi without a game book. Now, imagine his team characterized by failure and frustration, because that is what would have happened to the Green Bay Packers if their famous coach had not gone into the locker room with a strategy for winning. Every team that succeeds, that achieves its goals, does so because the leader charted a clear path. Employees are empowered, enabled to succeed, when their leaders give them a workable plan for success and the tools to implement it. Without plans, we have no means of measuring progress, no means of charting our accomplishments. Without a sense of accomplishment, we are marked with futility and discouragement—not the most flattering accessories for office wear.

🐝 Empowering means being flexible. It means adapting to unexpected changes among the staff or within the company at large. The leader's ability to make difficult adjustments on short notice gives her department employees reassurance when change might be otherwise unsettling, frightening. It gives them confidence to make adjustments too, to shift tasks, to rearrange priorities as needed, and to be flexible in their approach to the job. It has been said that that which is rigid breaks easily, and that which is flexible bends. Good leaders will empower their team by setting an example of bending when the wind blows change in their direction.

🐝 Empowering means continuing to learn and keep pace with the strides of industry. A good leader will study the business of her company and will share her knowledge with her staff. She will never assume she has learned all there is to know about her job or the work of a leader. She will make her employees' work easier by continuing to improve her own work. She empowers others by improving herself.

🐝 Empowering means accepting and submitting to constructive criticism from members of your team. It may seem inappropriate for the "boss" to allow his subordinates to be his critics, but good leaders will tell you it's not so. People in leadership are first and foremost *people*, and they will make mistakes—mistakes that are obvious to those who work closely with them. When a leader listens and accepts the critique of a worker, he aligns himself with the team and identifies himself with the common goals they share. By listening humbly and not reacting in anger, the leader proves his commitment to the effort of the whole; he demonstrates that his first priority is not personal gain at the expense of the team goal. When a leader acts quickly to correct his mistakes, he indicates that he is serious about achieving goals and he is not willing to let foolish pride interfere with the pursuit of excellence. Leadership combined with humility is a powerful combination. It not only empowers employees to be the best they can be, it also inspires in them greater respect for their leaders.

🐾 Empowering means allowing staff members to have ownership in their tasks. Research tells us that every human being has a basic drive to *own*, to possess or make a thing her own. As much as possible, a good leader will help her staff gain a sense of ownership in tasks, decisions, and plans for the future. She will ask for input when considering policy changes that will have wide impact. As partners in the decision-making process, employees can say, with honesty, "This was my idea, my decision." While employees can't make the final decision, they are usually more amenable to change when their thoughts and opinions have been given consideration at some point during the decision-making process.

🐾 Empowering means being well-rounded and balanced. Leaders who inspire their teams to excellence live lives that extend beyond the office. They have outside interests that give perspective to their work. Because they have other interests, hobbies, and family responsibilities, they encourage their employees to have a life outside the company, as well. They understand the value of such intangibles as relaxation, romance, recreation. Employees who work for such a leader are able to go home at quitting time without guilt. They are able to enjoy the weekend and return to the office on Monday with fresh energy. While office irritations may erupt, they are able to assign appropriate importance to petty problems. They understand that life is bigger than their prefab cubicle; it's bigger than charts and graphs; it's bigger than a computer monitor. Good leaders appreciate the ethic of work, but they have not forgotten how to play, and they don't want their employees to forget either.

🐸 Empowering means delegating. A good leader will never be heard saying, "If it's going to be done right, I'll have to do it myself." A good leader understands that delegating is an essential task of leadership. While there are few short-term benefits to delegation, the long term benefits are many:

🐸 Delegating teaches people how to perform major tasks that free the leader to do other tasks.

🐸 Delegating demonstrates the leader's trust in the employee and builds the employee's confidence.

🐸 Delegating gives the employee new, valuable skills that will, in the long term, be much more beneficial than if the leader had performed the task herself.

Good leaders will ask themselves these questions before delegating any task:

🐸 What tasks are best suited for delegation?

🐸 Why am I delegating these tasks?

🐸 To whom should I delegate these tasks?

🐸 What is a realistic time frame for the accomplishment of these tasks? Does the time frame allow time for critical feedback on the performance of the task?

While delegating, be sure the communication lines with your employees are in good working order. Give clear instructions and be willing to explain yourself and answer questions. Know the learning style of your employee—does she need to be shown? Does she learn more quickly if you demonstrate? Does she need "hands on" practice, allowing time for trial and error, before you cut her loose to work alone on the project?

And lastly, good leaders who delegate tasks know the importance of praise. While they will need to correct appropriately throughout the learning phase of the delegation process, they will not hesitate to compliment often.

🐾 The leader as a guide

Leaders serve as guides—whether in the office, the classroom, or the home. While they need knowledge and a bit of courage, they are not expected to be omnipotent nor omniscient. Their task is to choose a direction and to proceed forward, taking those who follow them to a desirable destination. In the office, that destination may be the top of the goal chart, or the conclusion and submission of a departmental project, or simply the daily execution of essential tasks. Whatever the destination, the leader, as guide, is in charge of the journey. I once heard a woman's account of her climb out of the rugged and remote Havasupai Canyon, a region of the Grand Canyon undiscovered until the early 1900s. She told about feeling alone and desolate on the hot, dusty path. Steep cliffs dropped off thousands of feet on one side of the narrow trail, and on the other side a granite wall seemed to reach up and skim cream off of milky clouds.

In some places, the path widened and opened into large areas where half a dozen trails darted off in different directions. And it was in those areas, where the route was unclear, that the woman searched for her guide. Each time, she found him several yards ahead, waiting in the sparse shade of a twisted pinion tree or leaning against a boulder the size of a truck.

She told of how relieved she felt at the sight of the old Indian man who had traveled the trails of the canyon since his childhood. At times, she thought, he seemed to sense her fatigue. As they trudged upward, he often turned around and glanced behind, catching her grimace as she glanced up at the distant canyon rim. He seemed to be able to read her thoughts, that the distance was too great, that the energy demanded for the climb was too much for her. At those times, he paused on the trail, waiting for her to catch up. Sometimes he pointed to a lizard sunning itself on a nearby rock, or the vivid burst of red in the blossom of an Indian paintbrush. And then, as though knowing that his charge had been nourished and renewed by the beauty along the way, he nodded toward the canyon rim and resumed the journey, turning his head often, listening for the crunching of footsteps in the gravelly path behind him.

For me, this story is a profound parable of leadership. It illustrates the importance of listening and paying attention to the needs of the ones we lead. Are we setting too hard a pace? Have we chosen the best route to the top? Have we paused to celebrate the small successes achieved along the way? Have we looked over our shoulders to see if anyone is with us on this journey toward the top? Or are we trudging on, so focused on our own private goals that we are unaware of the widening gap between ourselves and those who depend on our leadership?

The test of true leadership is found in the answer to a simple question: "Is anyone following?"

Perhaps those of us who fancy ourselves as leaders ought to pause a moment and listen for the sound of footsteps behind us. Perhaps we would do well to look over our shoulders and see if, indeed, anyone is following us toward a worthy goal.

CHAPTER 10

MISSION, VISION,
AND PASSION

"Thelma Wells, Assistant Vice-President."

I stared at the words engraved on the nameplate. They stared back at me from the edge of my executive-sized mahogany desk. A stack of mail lay on a plastic "in-box" in a disordered pile near my phone. Paper clips littered the top page of a yellow legal pad torn down to a thin tablet. Pink memo notes were strewn about, and the browning leaves of a thirsty philodendron plant trailed across the corner of the "out-box." All the trappings of corporate success, I thought.

It was 1984. No lap-top computers yet. No cellular phones. But as the officer in charge of the personal banking division, I managed to conduct business, nonetheless, and I never imagined I was ill-equipped. On the contrary, I felt as though I had everything necessary for success.

For four years, I had been serving as a bank officer and pursuing a business of my own on the side as a speaker/ teacher. My company, Thelma Wells and Associates, conducted workshops for banking trade organizations, such as the American Institute of Banking, as well as other financial institutions. I spoke on customer service and taught technical intricacies of banking. Now, after many months of building a substantial list of clients for myself, I had decided to leave the bank to pursue speaking and teaching full time.

It's a risk, I thought, as I looked around my office at the bank. If I leave here, I leave everything behind, I reminded myself for about the thousandth time. The desk, phone, office, not to mention a guaranteed salary every two weeks, plus a pension plan, medical benefits, and paid vacation—it all stays behind when I walk out. Can I really afford to shoulder all the costs of doing business?

It was a Friday afternoon, and I had come to work that day with the intention of tendering my resignation. All day I had struggled with myself. Should I do it? Should I wait another year, continue to build my client base before I leave?

George and I had talked about my leaving the bank many times in the four years since I'd formed Thelma Wells and Associates. He was encouraging and, because his business was thriving, we both felt the timing was right. Several times in recent weeks we had sat down with a pencil and pad and figured out all the math. On paper, it looked good, it looked plausible; but the thought of being completely on my own, with no guarantees, no promises of a paycheck—it was both terrifying and tremendously exciting.

Could I do it? Was my client base large enough?

"Let's go for it, hon," George had said.

It's now or never, I told myself that Friday afternoon. I took a deep breath and reminded myself that I had been preparing for this day for four years. I'd worked with a bank attorney to coauthor a new-accounts training manual for banks. I'd gathered credentials and experience carefully, calculating every speaking and teaching opportunity, weighing them against my goals to be self-employed. My entrepreneurial dream was close to fulfillment. With one final glance around the office, sparing a pitying thought for the dying philodendron, I got up and walked to the bank president's office to resign my position as assistant vice president. That was on Friday. Monday morning I returned to the bank and asked to meet with the vice-president in charge of employee training. I convinced him to hire me as a consultant to conduct workshops on customer service and training seminars for bank employees. Before I left the bank that day I deposited a $27,000 check in my corporate account—payment for a consultant's services twice weekly for the next four months.

For the next two years, I traveled throughout the state

to train employees in scores of financial institutions. I continued to teach classes at the American Institute of Banking. I worked long days, as well as nights and weekends, and I watched my income triple that of my banker's salary. But beginning in 1986, that income began to shrink.

As the banking empire in Texas foundered in the economic environment of the mid-eighties, my own personal empire also foundered. My largest consulting contracts were with banks, credit unions, and savings and loan institutions, and as they closed, one by one, insolvent, and many under federal investigation, my contracts became worthless. My current fees went unpaid, and past due accounts went into receivership. As more and more banks closed, I watched my business teeter on the edge of catastrophe.

All my contacts had been in the banking industry, so I had no other accounts to help keep my business alive. I had put all my eggs in a basket labeled "Banking," and now that basket lay crushed under the weight of unsecured loans, unscrupulous investments, and gross mismanagement.

At the same time my business was hovering dangerously close to bankruptcy, George learned that a planned freeway system was going to cut off traffic to his Mobil station.

"I'm going to lose the station, baby," George told me one night. He was a prophet, it seemed. Within a few months, the station closed, and George came home with a broken heart.

We're not quitters, I reminded myself often, as our family's financial house tottered.

George's people weren't quitters, and Grannie and Daddy Lawrence certainly weren't either. We're fighters, I told myself. We're survivors. We'll get through this somehow.

As I studied my company's dwindling accounts, I knew what I had to do. It was simple, really. I had to replace my banking clients with other clients. Only this time, I wouldn't limit myself to only one industry. This time, I would diversify.

I began by recreating myself. I could no longer afford to be perceived as a financial services expert. I had to broaden my image and enlarge my scope. Calling on all the energy and funds I could muster, I began marketing myself to businesses throughout the region, emphasizing my experience in teaching customer service. I offered to customize my workshops, tailoring my presentations to each customer's unique needs. I began writing and selling articles on a variety of business-related topics, putting my name before the reading public, and including copies of those articles in promotional packets I sent to potential customers.

I assessed my costs and my income needs and decided, if I was careful and extremely frugal, I could be more flexible in pricing my seminars. This simple, if somewhat painful, decision enabled me to market my services to small businesses and opened up entirely new sources of income to my company. In the past, when I was so focused on banks and credit unions and other financial institutions, I had ignored the potential of the small businessman or -woman. Now, I worked hard to court the interest of little neighborhood companies, as well as any other companies that might benefit from what I had to offer.

It was during this time of tearing down and rebuilding that I had the opportunity to assess myself and my dreams for my business. I asked myself questions that I had never before tried to answer.

So, all right, Thelma, I said to myself, Here's the deal: you can keep your company, earn a lot less than you'd like, and attempt to rebuild; or, you can give it up and go back into an employee position somewhere. Which is it going to be?

The answer was simple, and startling: I would keep my company and accept whatever income it generated.

I'm not in this for the money! I thought, surprised at this sudden realization. I do this because I love it!

I love interacting with a roomful of individuals, sharing ideas with them, helping them understand their industry and their individual responsibilities as employees. I love training them to do their jobs with excellence.

Sure, in the beginning, when the big checks were coming in and lucrative consulting contracts threw me into a higher tax bracket, the money was motivation. The money was fun! Later, however, when the money diminished, it was wonderful to realize that I was still having fun. With or without the big money, I liked my work. I looked forward to getting up every day. I had fun on the job.

That realization opened my eyes to the first of three important principles—principles I began to learn as I had to concentrate every thought, every effort toward saving my business and reestablishing it as a prosperous endeavor. I learned that passion is essential to success. Business owners and entrepreneurs cannot hope for success unless they pursue that which they feel passionate about. Secondly, those who achieve identify their mission; they define their reason for existence. And lastly, they state their vision, focusing their sights on goals and strategies for their success.

Passion

Passion for your product or service will energize you to crawl out of bed each morning, start the Chevy, merge into the morning traffic, and rush to your first appointment, even though there is no boss waiting for you with a time card. As an entrepreneur, you're your own boss now, and if you don't feel passionate about your business, you will find it hard (some find it impossible) to be disciplined in your work habits. Without passion, you'll find you have little reason to do the hard stuff of running a business, especially if the monetary rewards you expect are delayed or for any reason interrupted.

Passion for your work will push you to call just one more client before you quit for the day. If nine sales calls have proven futile, you will make that tenth call, because you are passionate about what you have to offer. You love your product, whether it's an item or a service, and you're convinced that the client will love it too. For me, one more call equals one more opportunity to schedule the workshops I'm so passionate about. One more call equals one more chance at success, and I want every chance I can get!

In the beginning, when I was first building my business, I felt passionate about my work. I took the extra jobs after working eight hours at the bank because I enjoyed teaching and speaking. The money was enjoyable too, but at that time it wasn't essential for my family's welfare. I still had a salary from the bank. It was later, when money was scarce, that love for my work made me keep pressing on, digging for clients in every kind of business setting. It was passion for my work that prevented me from giving it all up and looking for a job in a department store when the banking industry died. I wanted to speak and teach more than anything else. Passion produced perseverance and fueled my pursuit for success.

MISSION

Passion is essential, but by itself, it isn't enough to yield success. I learned this when I was faced suddenly with possible bankruptcy. In addition to passion, I needed a sense of *mission*. I needed to define what I was about, as a company. What was my purpose, my reason for existing? Without a sense of mission, I could not plot a course for success.

Prosperous business owners often spend a great deal of time, in the beginning, writing their "mission statement." In it, they articulate, as succinctly as possible, their purpose for being in business. More than merely a necessary step for incorporation papers, the exercise of writing a "mission statement" forces the company officers to think carefully about what they are in business for, and why.

As I sat down to prepare a promotions packet to send out to potential clients, I had to concentrate and structure my thoughts to create a clear, well-stated reason for my existence as a company. What is my mission, I asked myself?

What am I trying to accomplish?

The answer, for Thelma Wells and Associates, was fairly simple: My mission, as a company, was to inform, inspire, encourage, and educate people in the business environment, enabling them to pursue excellence, enabling them to be the best that they can be. My mission, put simply, was to extract diamonds out of dust.

That said, now all I had to do was figure out how I was

going to accomplish it. Now all I had to do was clarify my vision.

Vision

When I was forced to broaden my scope, I began to envision Thelma Wells and Associates as a company that could have worldwide impact. Thinking globally now, not regionally, or even nationally, I began to consider ways I could market my skills to international companies. I would travel to any city in the country, any city in the world, no region was too distant. What are borders and oceans, if not limits to be overcome?

My vision was also cooperative; I would join with other speakers and trainers, when appropriate. I would welcome the help and cooperation of other competent staff and people who would work efficiently and effectively with me to accomplish the mission of Thelma Wells and Associates. This was one of the best decisions I made. When an international seminar company offered to hire me as an independent contractor, I accepted. While I still worked to cultivate my own clients as well, the contract with the seminar company kept my business afloat. During the first two crucial years after the banks' demise, I had income from that contract, along with the freedom to pursue other business and rebuild my client base.

My vision was also long-range. I would proceed one day at a time, seeking to accomplish each day's goals, but I would also keep an eye on the distance ahead and be ready to make adjustments in my route as needed. I would look up, beyond the ground at my feet, and be prepared for changes as they occur. I would cultivate flexibility. I would keep an open mind and be willing to adapt and cooperate in the creation of opportunities along the way.

I'm convinced that business success, every kind of personal success, depends on the discovery of our individual passions and a clear understanding of our mission and our vision. But even with such discovery and clarity, success cannot be guaranteed. It is not a commodity that comes with a warranty if we're willing to pay the purchase price. Just ask Olympic champion Dan Jansen.

No athlete in recent history is more admired and respected than speed skater Dan Jansen. And no athlete in recent history has experienced more failure in a more public arena. Yet no one would accuse him of being dispassionate about his sport, unclear about his mission as an athlete, or shortsighted in vision.

Dan began skating as a child in Wisconsin, where he grew up in a close family, the youngest of nine children. All his life, he prepared for the Olympics, racing first in local events, proceeding to regional and finally to state events before finally winning national and world honors.

The 500 meter was Dan's event. By the time the 1988 Olympic games arrived, he was the recognized leader in his sport, the "greatest sprinter on long blades in the past decade," declared *Time* magazine. He came to Calgary the favorite. No one doubted that the skater from Wisconsin would take home a gold medal—maybe two. But on the day of his biggest race, his first Olympic competition, Dan self-destructed on the ice.

That day in Calgary, when he should have been filled with all the hope and confidence of a young, well-trained athlete already replete with honors and world records, Dan was filled instead with dread. His sister Jane was dying of leukemia, and he couldn't take his thoughts off her. He spoke to her by phone on the morning of his first race. It was the last time he would ever hear her voice. During the final hours before he was scheduled to skate, Dan learned of his sister Jane's death.

As he entered the rink for the most important race of his life, Dan's mind was dangerously divided between thoughts of his sister and thoughts of the oval sweep of the ice rink. While all the world watched his very public race, he ran a very private internal race against despair. In the end, grief tripped him and he fell in two races, losing the Olympic medal and flying home to bury his sister.

Four years later, Dan returned to the Olympics, arriving in Albertville, France, in 1992, fit for a medal, or more.

Faster than he'd ever been, stronger and more determined than before, he was fresh off a win at the World Cup, where he had set a new world's record for the 500 meter race. But he didn't reckon on the poor condition of the ice, or the complex mental and emotional conditions present inside him. He finished fourth, losing a medal by mere hundredths of a second. Dejected and confused, he skated the 1000 meter three days later, finishing in twenty-sixth place. Once again, Dan left the Olympics minus a medal, while all the world watched and wondered if he had what it takes to win the "big" one.

Dan was devastated by his losses at Albertville. Skaters and sports analysts all agreed that the condition of the ice influenced the outcome of the games, at least for the 500 meter race, but that was little solace to Dan. In his autobiography, he writes, "I knew what my critics were saying after Albertville: Dan Jansen was a choker. The two falls in Calgary could be explained by the death of his sister, but there was no explanation for Albertville, when he seemed to be an absolute lock for a medal."[1]

Two years later, at the 1994 Winter Games in Lillehammer, Norway, Dan came to the Olympics with a new vision and a new passion. His first race, the 500, went badly. But he had learned, through his coach, through his own body's responses, and through many hours with a sports psychologist, that the 1000 meter could be his. That he did, in fact, *love* that race. He entered the rink a believer.

Dan writes, "I felt powerful and smooth... I *love the 1000*... I just seemed to be sailing through the race, in complete control."[2]

In one frozen moment, on the second-to-last inner turn, with only 300 meters to go, Dan slipped. His balance faltered and his fingers skimmed the ice. Don't panic, he commanded himself, steadying himself and recovering quickly. But the watching crowd was already close to cardiac arrest, groaning in unison, dreading another loss for the athlete some writers had dubbed "the heartbreak kid."

Speaking to himself, repeating his coach's instructions and letting his body swing with the practiced rhythm of a speed skater, Dan raced on, pouring every molecule of his body's energy into every stride. He crossed the finish line the winner, setting a new world's record in addition to claiming the Olympic gold medal.

I love Dan's story. It's a vivid demonstration of what is required for success—success of any kind. Business owners as well as athletes have to face the reality of failure. All of us, at some time, will look into the face of tragedy and difficulty. We will have to make a choice: to return to the race, or to give up. If we choose the race, we may be forced to regroup, to redefine ourselves. And we will have to dredge up all the passion within us, digging deep for hidden reservoirs, if we are to persevere.

Often, difficulty and failure will force us to change our goals and realign our focus. We may have to adjust our vision, setting our sights on a new goal, the 1000 meter instead of the 500. Sometimes we have to shut our ears to the inner voices that would condemn us before we ever begin.

Those who achieve any measure of success understand that life is not static. It is a drama, with both comedy and tragedy, with plot twists and interesting characters and surprising outcomes. For all of us, entrepreneurs as well as speed skaters, and every worthwhile endeavor in between, there will be some slips and falls. But, as Dan wrote, "... you have to deal with them."[3]

How do you do that? By drawing on all the passion within you; by examining your mission, defining it or redefining it, if necessary; and by setting your sights on your goals, perhaps new goals, and by sharpening your vision of those goals.

For Dan Jansen, reestablishing himself as a world-class winner required the help of an experienced coach, many sessions with a sports psychologist, and the loving support of his extraordinary family. For you and me, our help may come from other sources, but one thing is certain: no matter how many people may wish to help us, we must do the hard work of perseverance ourselves. It is that which will enable us to recover from our failures.

No one could skate for Dan. His friends and family could cheer him on from the sidelines. His coach could shout instructions and oversee his training regimen; his psychologist could suggest ways to overcome negative thoughts. But only Dan could enter the rink. Only Dan could compete when the starting gun roared. Only Dan could cross the finish line.

Few of us are Olympic-caliber athletes, so let's bring Dan's lesson home to our environs. Here, where we work and chart our career paths, our families may encourage us from the sidelines—my husband, George, certainly did; our friends may believe in our skills and urge us to keep on trying—mine did. But Thelma Wells and Associates was *my* company. I *was* Thelma Wells. And I was the person who had to do the work of rebuilding after near-bankruptcy. I was the person who had to get up and keep trying, to go back to the disaster site, just as Dan had to return to the frozen rink.

Even the most prepared, the most dedicated, the most passionate among us face failure. But with every slip, every fall, a new opportunity appears: an opportunity to challenge ourselves and to redefine ourselves; an opportunity to broaden our scope and enlarge our vision; an opportunity to set new goals.

Slips and falls are common occurrences in the lives of ice skaters. Non-skaters like you and me take our share of falls too, don't we? But it helps to remember Dan's words, that how you deal with life's ups and downs makes all the difference.

There are no guarantees for success. But there is this guarantee: If, after falling, you don't get up and try again, you're sure to be left outside the winners' circle.

CHAPTER 11

I LOVE PEOPLE!

After his heartbreaking defeat at the 1992 Olympics, Dan Jansen worked for two years training and preparing for the moment when he would once again lace on his skates and try to erase the agony of his greatest athletic failure by claiming his greatest skating triumph—an Olympic gold medal. It took two years for my fallen company to regain its footing and rise to its feet again.

By 1988, Thelma Wells and Associates stood on solid financial ground. Not quite a world-class competitor, it was, however, getting stronger every day, and my vision of being a company of global dimensions didn't seem as far-fetched as it once did. I was soliciting clients with international subsidiaries, and I believed, I *knew*, in time, I would be traveling the world.

In the meantime, George showed mild interest in other business ventures. Our son graduated from high school and began studying to become a jeweler. He was accepted into an apprenticeship program and began designing his own pieces of fine jewelry. Lesa graduated from community college and beauty school and opened her own business. Vikki, now out of law school, was working in New York City and traveling the world whenever possible.

Our family had survived a serious economic fall. During the most difficult days, every member of the family had helped out in their own way. We had climbed back up on our feet, but I could see that my husband had sustained some injuries in the fall. Devastated by the loss of his station, he seemed dispirited, unenthusiastic about starting over again. He worked at starting new businesses that didn't satisfy him, even though they generated a fair income. And he grieved for the station he had lost.

To George, that station represented all that was good about the American way. Throughout his youth, before the civil rights movement gained momentum in this country, he had suffered and endured discrimination and the many indignities common to black men in America. When he purchased his own business in 1962 as a partner with Daddy Lawrence, he began to believe that perhaps there was something to recommend this system of government, even though for generations it had been a bitter enemy to many black men. For George, owning his own business was the ultimate freedom. The station on the corner of Second and Grand was the site of his liberty bell. It was there that he first experienced the pride of accomplishment and the pride of ownership. When the station was razed and a convenience store built on the site, some of his pride was buried as well.

Although my business was improving daily, I grieved for my husband's losses. I prayed for ways to encourage him, and I asked God to provide him with a new, satisfying career challenge. God's answer to that prayer lay a few years ahead, but in the meantime, I took heart as I saw George's interest in my company grow. When he wasn't on the job somewhere else, he offered to help me with mailings, errands, and many of the other myriad chores that I was trying to do myself.

In the beginning, to keep my business costs to a minimum, I worked out of our home, doing the work of secretary, marketing officer, accountant, and travel agent, and any other job that needed doing. In 1991, Vikki moved back to Dallas and began working with me in my business. She located a tiny office for me in the Small Business Incubation Center, and with all the family helping, we moved our files and desks into the space that would be home to my company for the next four years.

I will be forever grateful for the opportunity provided me by the efforts of Congresswoman Eddie Bernice Johnson, the Bill J. Priest Center for Economic Development, the Dallas County Community College District, and the Small Business Administration. Working together in a cooperative effort, these individuals and organizations created the Small Business Incubation

Center to help give small, minority-owned businesses a boost up the hill toward solvency and success. They offered inexpensive office space, the use of fax machines, computers, copiers, and other business services my very limited corporate budget couldn't have afforded otherwise.

What an exciting period that was in the life of my company. Vikki filled the position of marketing officer and aggressively pursued new accounts. Her knowledge of legal matters made her an invaluable asset, and her presence with me, working alongside me, was a pleasure I had never anticipated.

In 1993, in answer to my prayer, George announced that he wanted to join the family effort. He had endured three months of official retirement from the working world, and it was more than enough for him. He wanted to work at something worthwhile, something satisfying. He became part of the team, accepting the title of business manager, and working with me in sales and promotions.

Through all the changes and challenges, both the pleasant and the not so pleasant, I have tried to keep my vision for my company clear. As opportunities arrived, I continually laid them against the blueprint I had sketched for my company when I was forced to rebuild it or lose it. I continually reviewed my mission and assessed the level of my passion. I made the discovery that I was most effective when I was working in the area of human relations.

I was competent in other fields, such as training bank tellers (I still had a few banking clients), and I was quite capable of teaching courses on new accounts documentation, but I was at my best when I was working with people on relational skills.

This is what I'm really about! I thought, as I realized that I grew excited about researching and developing programs for people who must interact with other people in order to do business. I loved writing and conducting workshops to teach people how to serve their customers, how to relate to their co-workers, how to get along with difficult people, how to develop negotiating skills (particularly secretaries), how to apply common sense strategies for managing stress, and how to understand and function well in a culture stamped by diversity.

I loved motivating and encouraging people. I loved inspiring them to move beyond mediocrity, to move beyond the limits of "we've always done it that way." I loved helping them discover new tools for building bridges instead of walls. I loved watching people apply new skills and increase their sense of self-esteem, along with their employer's profits.

The bottom line was, I loved people. Working with them afforded me instant gratification. I could present them with an idea or a technique that instantly opened their eyes to new prospects, new potential for personal growth as well as corporate growth. And for that, people would pay me money!

What a life! What a satisfying, enjoyable life.

As I worked on seminars, doing research and developing programs, I realized that much of my work focused on how to motivate people in positive ways. Employers were always interested in how they could bring out the best in their employees, how they could generate positive attitudes, how they could encourage a more cooperative spirit within a department or company, how they could inspire a staff to reach for the highest level of accomplishment.

"How can we motivate our team, Thelma?"

Sales managers ask that question; customer service managers ask that question; warehouse supervisors ask that question; company CEOs ask that question. And I always answer, "People don't lack motivation. Everything we do is a response to some kind of motivation. The problem is that too often we are responding to negative motivation. The challenge to all of us is this: to activate *positive* motivation."

Negative stimuli are all around us. Fear, anxiety, self-pity—these are factors that can motivate us to react to life, to challenges and difficulties, even to pleasant events, with negative behavior.

The responsibility of a good leader, in the home or on the job, is to replace negative motivation with positive motivation.

As I've studied human behavior and its relationship to motivation, I've noticed that the same things that motivate me also motivate everybody else. For all of us, positive motivation results when we are made to feel appreciated, loved, valued, and important. And the results are a job well done and a satisfied employee. But beware the worker operating on a supply of negative motivation.

It is easy to spot individuals whose behavior is fueled by negative factors. They will demonstrate any number of irritating symptoms, such as grumpiness, hostility, inflexibility, and resentment of criticism or any kind of feedback. Their work record will reveal missed deadlines, absenteeism, tardiness, poor work relationships, and low productivity.

These symptoms aren't limited to the workplace. Many people cope with these behaviors in the home as well, where simple, straightforward solutions may be difficult to implement because families are often emotion-charged. But there are remedies, and they can work in almost any environment.

Activating positive motivation in individuals, both at home and at work, requires the leader or manager (or parent/ authority figure) to do three things. First, a manager must create the right climate; second, she must set purposeful and meaningful goals; and, third, she must be sure the system in which others must work is a helpful one.

Let's look at each of these three "must do's" in more detail (and remember, we're talking about positive motivation now).

🐾 Create the right climate.

People are motivated to work, and to work well, when they have freedom to act on their own initiative. That means the leader is not a control freak who must have ultimate control over every tiny task in the office. Nothing is more stifling to us than being observed and scrutinized by someone who is obsessive about petty, insignificant things.

People are motivated in positive ways when their manager sets high expectations for performance. Is it reasonable to demand enthusiasm and excellence from a worker whose supervisor is expecting a poor, sloppy job from him? In work, as in life, we tend to sink, or rise, to the level of expectations assigned to us.

People are motivated when their individual gifts and skills are respected. Managers who recognize and praise the accomplishments of their employees are nurturing an environment where productivity and office morale can grow. Appreciation always yields worthwhile rewards.

People are motivated when they are encouraged to express their creativity and to try innovative techniques. Unlike robots, human workers have great potential for conceiving new ideas, new ways of performing routine tasks. Good managers understand this and allow workers to experience the exhilaration and satisfaction of creative thought. They allow as much flexibility and experimentation as possible, while keeping a careful eye on matters of safety and time management. The workers in this kind of a climate will be looking for ways to do the job better.

People are motivated when they feel like they are a part of a team effort. It's not cliche to say that no man or woman is an island. A healthy environment encourages unity and the pursuit of common goals, while allowing each person to see that their contribution is vital to the whole.

🐾 Set meaningful goals.

People are motivated when they are given reasonable goals, goals that are attainable. Asking the impossible only ensures failure and weakens the will to achieve.

People are motivated when they are given challenging goals, goals that indicate their leader recognizes their intelligence and their capabilities. Respect is always a positive motivating factor.

🐾 Create a helpful system in the workplace.

People are motivated when the system, or the orderly structure for conducting business in the office (or the home), allows for open communication, where feedback and evaluation are available.

People are motivated when that system operates in a consistent manner, under reasonable controls, and when, they know what to expect in any given situation. Inconsistency hinders positive motivation. It creates confusion and uncertainty—two large stumbling blocks destined to trip up travelers on the path toward achievement.

Most discussions about motivation involve the use of the word "excellence." It seems every company, every family, wants something more than just smooth operation and a record of average accomplishments. They want excellence.

We want excellence. We want to know how to motivate people to reach higher, to achieve more, to break all performance records. Simple efficiency is not enough. We want stardom.

Such aspirations are admirable, in their place, as long as the pursuit of excellence does not become confused with the pursuit of perfection.

I've already confessed to being a recovering perfectionist. I remind myself often that demanding perfection—whether of myself or of others—always yields negative results. When I demand perfection, I guarantee disappointment. When I demand perfection, I can expect discouragement. When I demand perfection, disillusionment is what I'll get instead.

Through the years, I've noticed that when I expect or demand perfection of people, I see futility in their eyes. They give up quickly, feeling doomed to failure. Or, they refuse even to try, knowing before they ever begin that the job will not be acceptable to me.

When I demand perfection, I set up the conditions for failure. I pile a heavy weight of stress on others, contributing to the factors that cause illness.

When I urge others to pursue excellence, a very different combination of factors is put to work. They experience self-satisfaction, and their stress load is decreased. They are able to work with freedom, willing to risk trying new techniques and to explore new ideas; they are able to get over mistakes quickly and begin again, because they have been allowed to learn from their errors rather than suffer for them.

Human beings have a built-in resistance to the demand for perfection. We know we cannot achieve it, and it angers us to have someone require it of us. And anger is seldom a welcomed presence either in the workplace or the home.

While it is unreasonable to expect perfection in any form, we do have the right to expect competence and a degree of excellence when we venture into the marketplace. We have the right to expect fair treatment and efficient service from sales people, service people, and any other kind of worker whose salary or hourly wage we support with our own hard-earned dollars.

When we step up to the sales counter, or the bank teller's window, or enter the accountant's office, or sit in the dentist's chair, we have a right to expect those serving us to be motivated and attentive to our needs. After all, we're paying for their services.

Sometimes our expectations go unmet. Sometimes a simple business transaction becomes a nightmare. That's what happened to me late one night in Washington, D.C.

It all started when my flight from Houston arrived at National Airport nearly two hours later than scheduled. I fought my way through the corridors of the airport, dragging my luggage, and stepped up to the counter of the rental car company, puffing as if I'd just been disconnected from an oxygen tank.

The only clerk on duty was a young woman of about twenty-five. She stood with her back to me, fussing with someone over the phone. I waited only a few seconds before I tapped on the counter and spoke up, "Miss? Oh, miss? Can you help me here?"

The woman glanced over her shoulder, the phone still pressed to her ear.

"I have a car reserved, and I have to have it right now," I said.

The woman frowned. With deliberate slowness, she hung up the phone and sauntered over to the counter, positioning herself behind the computer.

"I need a credit card," she said, flitting her fingers over the computer keys.

"No, no, you see, the car was reserved by the company that hired me," I explained. "I'm not supposed to have to give you a credit card. Just type in my name and my driver's license number and the confirmation number.

The profile will give you the information you need," I told her.

"I can't rent you a car without your card, lady," the woman said, fixing a bored look on me.

"I know you usually get a card when you rent a car, but I was told to just give you my name and driver's license number and everything you need would show up on the computer," I said.

The woman continued to stare at me, doing nothing.

"I need a credit card," she said, speaking slowly and enunciating each word as if I hadn't been smart enough to understand her when she said it the first time.

"No, you see, the car isn't being charged to me, it's being charged to the company that hired me," I said, breathing deeply, forcing calmness into my voice.

"What's your name?" the woman asked.

"Thelma Wells," I replied. "You should show a reservation for me. Here's my driver's license and the confirmation number."

"I said I need a credit card," the woman said, sighing and leaning on the counter in a lazy manner. "I can't do anything without a credit card."

I could feel heat crawling up my neck. I glanced around, wondering if it would be easier to walk to another car rental company and start the whole business over again. I didn't have time to fight with this woman much longer.

"Look," I said, my chest tightening, exasperation nearly choking me, "Are you going to listen to me or not? I've got to have that car and I've got to have it now, understand?"

What the clerk didn't know was that I was in real danger of being stranded on the side of the road in the remote town of Indian Head, Maryland. It was a tiny place, unused to frequent travelers, and it had only one motel. Vikki had spoken to the owners when she reserved me a room.

"Mom, they normally close at 10:00 p.m.," Vikki had told me, "but they have agreed to wait until midnight in case your plane is late. They won't stay open a minute past twelve, so if you're late, plan on sleeping in your rent car," Vikki had warned, half-joking.

There I stood at the car rental agency in Washington, D.C., and it was already nearly midnight, and I wasn't laughing. It would take at least an hour and a half to drive from Washington, D.C., to Indian Head. If I didn't get that rental car and leave immediately, the motel—the only one in town—would be closed, and I would have to sleep in the car.

A lone, middle-aged woman asleep in the back seat of a rental car parked alongside the road—it was not a picture I cared to contemplate.

As every second ticked by I grew more agitated and more angry. My heart pounded, and I felt myself release the grip I'd been holding on my temper.

"Listen, woman," I growled, leaning toward her across the counter, "I'm going to get a rental car and I'm going to Indian Head if I have to take you with me!"

The woman frowned and, blinking, she took a quick backward step. I leaned further across the counter, my hands gesturing and pointing wildly.

"You don't know me, but I travel all over the world telling people how to do their jobs, and I'm going to tell your boss a thing or two if you don't GET ME MY CAR!"

Suddenly, a door opened behind the woman and a tall, handsome young man walked out.

"Can I help you, ma'am?" he said in a voice that could only be described as cajoling.

"Yes, you can!" I bellowed. "I need a car and I need it right now. I've got to get out of here in the next two minutes or I'm going to be sleeping in that car on the side of the road."

"Yes, ma'am," he said, nodding and offering a faint smile.

"If you think I'm loud and angry right now, just keep me waiting here a few minutes longer and you'll see somethin' that's not pretty, you understand me?" I threatened.

He nodded again.

"You don't know who I am!" I shouted. "I'm Thelma Wells, and I teach customer service all over the world. I teach people how not to get angry when they deal with people like you!"

"I'll have you out of here right away, ma'am," the man answered in a calm voice, and he motioned for the woman to step aside. With quiet efficiency, he approached the computer and began typing. In mere seconds, he said, "I'm sorry, Mrs. Wells. I do have your car. If you'll come with me, I'll take you to it right now."

He picked up my bags and escorted me through the terminal to where rental cars were parked. All the while we walked, I talked, giving him my seminar on how to teach people to be more sensitive to the needs of customers, how to go the extra mile to help, even in unusual circumstances—even if they don't want to supply a credit card.

We stopped at a dark-toned compact car, and the man unlocked the doors, stashed my luggage and briefcase in the back seat, and gave me directions to the highway that would take me to Indian Head, Maryland. Before I drove away, he apologized again and wished me a good trip and a successful business meeting. His quiet, considerate manner was beginning to have a calming effect on me, but twenty miles into the trip I could still feel my heart's too-rapid beating and my neck was still hot and burning. It's a good thing he came along when he did, I thought, remembering how close I'd come to leaping over the counter and slapping that silly woman.

All right, I wouldn't have leaped over the counter, and I wouldn't have slapped her, but my state of mind had been quickly approaching the frenzied level, and I was feeling desperate. I had already begun mumbling that I would never do business with that rental agency again. I was considering how many nasty letters I could write to the corporate headquarters. And I'd mentally noted the name of the woman who had been so rude, so indifferent to my needs.

Now I was trying to remember the name of the nice man who had emerged from the office, as if from a phone booth. At that moment, he could have been wearing a cape and tights and a huge red "S" on his chest.

"Now, that man is an example of someone who's motivated to do his job and to do it with excellence," I said, talking out loud to the empty car. "I'll use him in one of my workshops," I added. "He's good material."

I turned up the volume on the radio and checked a map to be sure I was on the right road to Indian Head. I watched the digital clock in the dashboard as the lighted

125

numbers flashed and midnight gleamed closer and closer.

That woman! I thought. If I have to sleep in this car...

How could she have been so insensitive to my needs? I thought, feeling a fresh wave of anger and frustration.

I arrived in Indian Head, Maryland, late, an hour and a half past midnight, and found the motel office locked and dark. After banging on the door a few times, I gave up and climbed back into the car and sank against the seat, exhausted and frightened. My head was throbbing and my stomach churning. What am I going to do? I thought.

At that moment, a woman came out of one of the motel rooms and walked toward a coke machine that stood near the office. She was startled when I called out to her.

"No, there's no other motel in town," she told me, when I asked about someplace else to stay.

"Could you let me use a blanket?" I asked. "It looks like I'm going to have to sleep in my car."

"No, I can't," she answered without apology.

I was too tired to argue or demand.

"Look," she said, "if you drive through town and turn right at the first signal, the road will take you to another town about forty miles away. There's a motel there. You might be able to get a room."

An hour later, after a frightening drive through narrow, poorly lit country roads, I saw the blinking sign for a Motel 8. A desk clerk rented me a room, and I threw myself onto the bed, too tired to take off my clothes. I slept for a couple of hours before I had to get up and shower and begin the drive back to Indian Head for the seminars scheduled for 8:00 a.m.

My audience in Indian Head was comprised of Naval and civilian personnel. I was their guest, invited to motivate them and encourage them in their tasks. I was expected to be "up!"

I had to put the awful ordeal of the night before out of my thoughts and think about being enthusiastic, funny, positive, and informative. No stories of torture and terror for this group.

But later audiences heard every horrifying detail of the nightmare at the rental agency.

I often tell that experience in my workshop on customer service to illustrate one employee's total contempt for the needs of a customer and another's extra effort to accommodate a customer (he didn't have to carry my luggage to the car for me). And I add myself to the cast of players in that late night drama.

I was the difficult customer. I had reasons for my behavior, and these too were important. I had come to the counter operating under negative stimuli: fear—who wants to sleep in the car on the side of the road in a strange town? And anxiety—will I be able to find this small town, alone, in the darkness, late at night? Fatigue—it had already been a very long day, and it wasn't over yet. Loss of control—someone else held the keys to the car I needed and it seemed nothing I could do would release them.

"I'm an expert in personnel relations!" I'd shouted at the woman behind the rental agency counter. "I know when people aren't behaving right, and lady, you're out of line. Now give me the keys to my car and get out of my way!"

Some expert.

At that time, I was nothing more than a disgruntled customer whose expectations of service were not being met. And, to be fair, the woman behind the counter had expectations of her own: she expected to transact business as usual. To her, that meant requesting a credit card.

On both sides of the counter, expectations went unmet. My sense of urgency fueled conflict. My state of mind, already disheveled by worry, interfered with even the possibility of reasonable discourse.

Looking back, it's easy to see that the WIIFM factor was in place and operating at full capacity that night. "What's In It For Me?" is always a factor in a discussion that relates to motivation. For the woman who was responsible for providing service, it was not so easy to change her method of operation. Her job security depended upon her doing the job right, the way she had been trained. In order for her to deviate from the way she had been taught, she had to be convinced it would be beneficial for her, or, at the least, that it wouldn't harm her.

In her defense (I can afford to be generous now, now that the urgency of the situation has passed), she was trying to be efficient, but she failed to be effective.

When it comes to customer service, efficiency must always be measured against effectiveness. And effectiveness must always be considered in terms of excellence.

Someone once wrote that excellence is attained if you:

Care more than others think is wise;
Risk more than others think is safe;
Dream more than others think is practical;
Expect more than others think is possible.

(Unknown)

The young man who rented me the car and carried my bags didn't share his dreams with me, but I'm sure he had visions of advancement. It was obvious to me that he was willing to risk more than the woman at the counter. In order to provide service to me, an unhappy customer, he broke with the traditional way of doing business. He cared more about serving a customer than about the order in which data is entered into the computer. His actions may have seemed unwise to his co-worker, but to me, the customer, they were life-saving.

What were his motives that night? What was in it for him?

Only two people were there to observe his behavior. The woman at the counter wouldn't have faulted him if he'd told me to take my business elsewhere—she was ready to do that herself. And if I'd written a letter to complain to his supervisor, surely someone up the corporate ladder would have come to his defense. After all, the crazy lady didn't even offer a credit card, and everybody knows rental transactions are *always* conducted with a credit card.

So, what motivated the employee to come to my aid? What motivated him to decide to conduct business in a way that was contrary to the normal procedure? Why did he come out from the behind the counter, escort me to the car, carry my bags, unlock the doors, see me settled in the driver's seat, and make sure I understood the directions to my destination?

I was a total stranger, one he would probably never see again. It was late at night, and there were few people standing about ready to applaud his good deeds. He had little to gain by such a dramatic show of service. Knowing all this, there can be only one explanation for his extraordinary actions: The man cared.

He cared about me. He cared about the reputation of his company. He cared about his job performance. He cared about standards of excellence.

How often have we heard it said that folks just don't seem to "care" about service the way they used to? We've all had a few experiences in the marketplace that would make us believe that there might be a measure of truth in that statement. But how wonderful it is to find service providers in every industry that contradict that impression. These are the employees who give exceptional attention to their customers by demonstrating extraordinary effort, by expressing genuine concern for a job well done.

Like the agent at the car rental counter, most of them perform without benefit of an audience. They do their work with excellence, not because someone is watching and waiting to reward them with an ovation, but because it is the only way they know how to do the job.

These people inspire me. When the motivator needs motivation, these are the people I remember.

My work, on a platform, in front of crowds, often draws applause, laughter, and kind words of appreciation. But without the excellent work of other, less visible, service providers, I would not be able to do my job. Professional service providers make my travel arrangements—and often make last minute changes. They rent me cars (with or without a credit card), check my baggage, vacuum my hotel room, serve my meals, and attempt to meet my needs as a consumer in hundreds of ways every day.

They seldom, if ever, hear the lovely sound of hands clapping in appreciation. They get few hugs and handshakes of appreciation, and yet they do their jobs well and with enthusiasm, and they make it possible for me to do mine. For that, I consider them heroes.

They may not own a pair of ice skates and an Olympic medal, but like Dan Jansen, they've learned the hard lessons and they understand the value of positive motivation. While their diligence and accomplishments will never win them a commercial endorsement or the chance to be grand marshal in a parade, they faithfully pursue excellence, most of them in anonymity, and many for minimum wage.

Make room for these, Dan. They, too, are nothing less than world class. And I love each and every one of them.

CHAPTER 12

THE MEASURE OF SUCCESS

I was walking down the church steps one Sunday when my friend, Mary Jo Evans, stopped me and admired the gold bee pinned on the lapel of my suit.

"Thelma Wells, that sure is a pretty bee," she said. "Every time you wear that, remember that you can 'be-ee' the best at whatever you want to 'be-ee.'" She stretched out the one syllable word, smiling as she spoke. I couldn't mistake her meaning.

That's it, I thought. That's the symbol I've been looking for, and it's been pinned on my shoulder all this time.

I'd been conducting seminars and lecturing about success for several years. I'd been on the lookout for a logo I could use to represent my theme. I needed a handle people could grab hold of—something they could take with them as a reminder when they left my seminars and returned to the workplace. That day, Mary Jo gave me the idea to use the bumblebee as my symbol.

The fact that scientists and aeronautical engineers can't explain the unlikely flight of the bumblebee makes it an even more appropriate symbol for me. The black illegitimate child of a crippled teenager, born more than two decades before the passage of the Civil Rights Bill—why would anyone expect her to get off the ground? It didn't take me long to fit the bumblebee metaphor into my workshops.

In my seminars, I began presenting an acrostic of the word "BEE" to represent the ingredients necessary for success:

B   Be aware of who you are. Know your vision, your mission, your passion. Know who you are, what you want, and how badly you want it.

E 🐝 Eliminate negative influences, accentuate the positives. Search for quality and solutions.

E 🐝 Expect the best from yourself and from others.

Thanks to the loving influence of Grannie and Daddy Harrell, and Daddy Lawrence, and the many other people who invested generously in me, these principles have been at work in my life for many years. But I continue to learn from them. And just like everyone else, I often struggle with them. Knowing what I should do and then doing it is a constant challenge, not only in the workplace, where I am Thelma Wells and Associates, a speaker and teacher, but also in the larger world and in the home, where I am just Thelma Wells.

"Being the best you can be" isn't limited to job performance. Being the best that you can be is of little value unless it begins on the personal level and extends into every area of our lives.

Albert Einstein said, "Try not to become a man of success but rather a man of value."

Success, *true* success, is demonstrated by the integrity of the total life. It transcends professional performance and on-the-job achievements. Its finest definition is found in a man's or woman's character. It is expressed most dramatically in the context of personal relationships.

It's not enough to be the best office manager you can be. It's not enough to be the best salesman you can be, or the best bank teller, or the best secretary, or the best at any career choice. It's not enough for me to be the best seminar leader I can be, or the best motivational speaker I can be. Each of those titles represents what I *do*. It is what I *am* that shows the true measure of my success.

The motivational speaker steps down from the podium; the secretary hangs up the phone and rushes for the elevator; the company president walks out of his suite of offices; the building manager locks the doors and goes home. The workplace is emptied as homes fill with men and women called "Mom" and "Dad", instead of "Sir" and "Ma'am." Titles stay at the office. At home, in the community, we are simply men and women, mothers and fathers, husbands and wives, sons and daughters, friends and neighbors—people who will demonstrate the level of our integrity to those closest to us.

It is here, among our most intimate companions, that we reveal what it really means to BEE the best that we can be.

I'll confess: these are the areas of greatest challenge for me. At home, no one applauds when I speak. Recently, my son George commented, "Everybody ought to listen to my mother... I wish I had." For years, he didn't. Most children don't—until they aren't children anymore.

At home, I get few hugs for vacuuming the hallway or unloading the dishwasher. These are chores that need doing. On the road, members of my audiences often hug me after I've done my job.

At home, or in my neighborhood, mediating conflict is seldom rewarded with a pat on the back and the words, "Well done, Thelma." It's expected behavior. But in Atlanta, or Dallas, or Washington, D.C., corporate executives thank me (and pay me) for doing my part to help deal with disputes in the workplace.

At home, at church, in line at the post office or the grocery store, at a homeowners' meeting, I'm not Thelma Wells and Associates. I'm Thelma Wells—woman, wife, mother, daughter, sister, neighbor, and friend. As Thelma Wells, *person,* I have to invest great effort into applying the principles I teach. I have to remember each letter of the acrostic and put into practice what I preach in the workplace. I must work at being the best woman that I can be, when there is no audience, no applause, and no paycheck.

Sometimes, *most* times, that is the hardest kind of "best" we can be. There are no salaries, no year-end bonuses for an exceptional show of friendship. We don't hear about commissions paid to daughters or sons or fathers or mothers for their lifelong investment of kindness and loyalty. Compassion is not rewarded by a gold watch. Yet, these are priceless traits of the truly successful human being, regardless of his or her professional status. And often, the effort and hard work associated with such success is more grueling than the kind we sweat and labor for in the workplace.

BE AWARE

Awareness is an important first step in our advance toward success in our professional lives: awareness of our vision, our mission, and our passion; awareness of who we are as individuals in the corporate setting; awareness of our skills and our aptitudes. In order to be successful outside the boardroom, beyond the job site, we must have that same kind of awareness. We must become aware of who we are and what we are about, as people who are both unique and complex.

Not long ago, while packing for a trip to Singapore and Australia, I went looking for my passport. When I found it buried under some papers in a file drawer, I opened it and checked the renewal date. Still valid, I noted, and then, before stuffing it into my purse, I studied my photo. Not quite as bad as my driver's license, I thought.

Just holding my passport that day dredged up a bushel of unpleasant memories of the time years earlier when I'd first attempted to apply for one. A clerk at the passport office had instructed me to bring my birth certificate as proof of U.S. citizenship when I came in to fill out the paperwork. After a frustrating search, I discovered that no record existed for a child named Thelma Smith. What I did find, however, was an official document declaring the birth of a child called "Baby Girl Morris."

Imagine the confusion when I tried to establish my identity as Thelma Smith Wells. Not until I'd gone to court to legally change my name from "Baby Girl Morris" to Thelma Wells was I able to fill out the paperwork for a passport. The legal ordeal, the cost, the confusion, the paper chase—the whole experience of establishing my identity underscored the wide chasm that existed between me and the woman who had given me birth but never named me. It was a chasm I had not been willing to acknowledge for a very long time.

It is an interesting coincidence that while I was sorting through the legal matter of changing my name, my mother began phoning me after a period of silence. I wasn't sure how to respond to her tentative efforts at conversation. Our visits were brief, casual—we'd been apart for so many years it was impossible to talk to each other with the intimacy of a mother and daughter.

It was the same with my sister, Sarah Elizabeth. Too many years separated us. We had been apart since adolescence, each inhabiting our separate worlds, each a little uncertain about how to communicate with each other. But suddenly, about that same time, she was there, wanting to be a part of my life, and I wasn't sure how to receive her.

Grannie was gone, my own children were grown, and I was fighting a depressing sense of isolation. My odd birth certificate had prompted me to wonder, Who was Baby Girl Morris? Who was the woman who gave her life and then handed her over to someone else to raise? I struggled with these and other disturbing questions.

What about Grannie? She was the mother who had raised me. By genetics, I belonged to my birth mother, but my heart would always belong to Grannie Harrell.

Grannie had been "mother" to me. She had bandaged my hurts and mopped my tears. She had disciplined me and praised me and encouraged me. I would always think of her as my mother. So, what could I give to the woman who had given birth to me? Could I love her as I had loved Grannie? Would I be betraying Grannie if I allowed my mother to enter my life at this late date? And if I let her into my life, would she ask more of me than I could give? While I struggled with these contrary thoughts, I was also troubled by how little I knew my mother, and I was aware of an emptiness because of her absence.

Shortly after my mother began calling me, her health began to decline. Our conversations underwent a change. I sensed in my mother a need for something more than courtesy, something more than civil conversation over the phone. It wasn't merely a friendly acquaintance she wanted. She wanted family intimacy. She wanted the love of a daughter. I wasn't sure I could give her that.

"I never gave you away," my mother insisted, when she spoke of my life with Grannie. It was important to her that I understand that. I thought about my mother, an unmarried teenager, crippled and uneducated, handing her baby over to a strong woman who would ensure the child a safe and nurturing childhood. I realized her sacrifice as I considered my own children. Would I have been able to let someone else raise them if my own circumstances would have caused them to suffer?

My sister Sarah had stayed with Mother, but her life had taken a much different route. Their home had not had been a stable one, like Grannie's and Daddy Harrell's. Exposed to harsher realities as a child, Sarah's innocence was snatched away when she was very young. Often alone and vulnerable, she grew up without the sense of safety that enfolded me. The early childhood visits we shared as little girls ceased when we entered our teens. It wasn't until many years later, when we were both middle-aged adults, that we connected again, and the love we'd known as children was rekindled.

We had to work at it, to reach out to each other and find ways to make that connection. As adults, we discovered we share common goals and values: We both love our children; we've embraced the same faith; and we both love to go out to eat. Over the last few years, we have united in the effort to care for our aging mother.

Sometimes gaining awareness is like putting on a pair of new shoes. Even though the size is right, they may feel uncomfortable, too snug, the leather too stiff. You know your options: you can kick them off, and step out unprotected, or you can walk in them awhile, knowing that the longer you own them the more comfortable they will become.

Focusing on the distance that separated me from my mother and my sister brought many uncomfortable feelings to the surface—feelings that revealed deep, unaddressed longings to know them better and to make peace with whatever conflicts divided us.

Two thousand years ago, Jesus told his disciples and a crowd of thousands who gathered to hear his first recorded sermon, "Blessed are the peacemakers, for they shall be called the sons of God."[4]

For all of us, there comes a time when we must make peace with life. That peacemaking is always preceded by awareness, and it always yields blessedness.

Blessedness is an old word we don't use much anymore,

but its meaning carries a sense of well-being and contentment. As I embarked on the serious task of peacemaking with my sister Sarah Elizabeth and my mother, I began to experience that blessedness Jesus spoke of. The relationship we share has enriched my life immeasurably. I cannot imagine a week passing without seeing them, talking with them, and enjoying the pleasure of their company.

Awareness is an ongoing exercise. As I learn about my mother and my sister, and as our bond strengthens, I'm becoming more aware of how much alike we are. As illness takes its toll on my mother, I'm learning the strength of my faith and the depth of the love I have for her. And I'm becoming more and more aware of all that I have to be thankful for.

ELIMINATE THE NEGATIVES;
ACCENTUATE THE POSITIVES

Successful people have made the deliberate decision to eliminate negative influences from their lives. They've decided to forget past wrongs, or at least refuse to dwell on them. They've chosen to associate with individuals who are not destructive. They've assessed themselves, acknowledged their weaknesses, and made the decision to accentuate their strengths. It is a deliberate choice, requiring that we aggressively search for quality, that we never give up the quest for solutions. This is true in the marketplace, where we strive for professional success. It is also true on the personal level.

Sometimes, oftentimes, making this kind of choice results in some pretty dramatic changes: An angry, rebel-ready youth, on the verge of taking the low road, the one that leads into juvenile hall, becomes an enthusiastic, willing student with visions of success and achievement; a dour, slow-speaking, shuffle-walking girl is transformed into a witty, ambitious, energetic young woman who views life as a wonderful adventure.

I've seen this kind of transformation.

It was a warm summer day in Texas, and I was visiting in the home of a friend I'll call Beth. That day, as on many other days, she was grieving over a young woman who was very dear to her. Our conversation was interrupted by the sound of a screen door slapping against its frame. When I looked up, a slouching girl with a vacant, despairing look on her face shuffled into the room.

Beth introduced us and then added, "Laurie, what a coincidence. We've just been talking about you."

Beth didn't have to tell me this was the girl we'd been discussing. Everything about her—her posture, her manner, her expression—identified her. She dropped down in an overstuffed chair and began complaining. In her voice I heard the sound of an angry, disappointed girl who believed she'd been dealt a lousy hand: her latest job had ended with a dismissal; a recent job interview had ended badly; her mother had disappointed her; her marriage was a disaster; and on and on...

Beth and I listened to Laurie recount her failures and disappointments. Life was crummy, but it wasn't her fault. Things just seemed to go wrong for her. She blamed her husband, her employers, and everyone else who came to mind, but the major villain in her tragedy was her mother.

"She didn't spend enough time with me," Laurie said, sighing. "She wasn't there for me when I was younger."

"She's there now, Laurie," Beth countered. "She loves you very much and reaches out to you constantly."

"If she'd been around before, my marriage might be better," Laurie whined.

"I know she wants to do what she can now," Beth said.

"I don't know what I'm going to do about a job," Laurie moaned. "Every time I start working something goes wrong. You know, my mother was never a good example for me. She never could hold a job for very long."

The litany of life's disappointments droned on. Finally, my friend Beth leaned forward in her chair and, grabbing Laurie's hands, she said, "Laurie, you can't spend your life rehearsing all the disappointments you've experienced. No one has had a perfect life," she said. "I know your mom, and she's given you every thing she has to give for several years now. Why must you always forget that?"

"Yes, but, before... " Laurie began.

"Before is over," Beth said. "Forget it. Now, today, you

have many positives to focus on. Try thinking about those for a change."

Laurie had never heard Beth speak to her like that before. She sat quietly for a moment, looking down at her hands.

Beth continued.

"Laurie, you can go on remembering every past hurt, every negative experience, every disappointment, or you can decide to concentrate on the positives in your life. You've got a good education, sweet children, and a mother who tries to show you how much she loves you. If you choose to ignore all that, you're going to be miserable and unfulfilled all your life."

I had listened in silence throughout the conversation, but at this point, Beth looked at me and said, "Thelma, you make a living talking about this kind of thing. What do you have to add?"

"You've just about said it all, Beth," I answered. "It's true, Laurie. Focusing on the negatives in life is going to hinder you from ever gaining any kind of success. That includes success in your marriage, in your home, as well as in job situations."

"I can't just change everything that happened in the past," Laurie mumbled. I knew she was still thinking of her mother's years of alcoholism and the years of neglect. She was still placing blame.

"You can change the present and the future, Laurie," I told her. "You can decide to take responsibility for yourself and your own happiness, and the future will be different.

"You know about good work habits—don't blame anyone but yourself if you lose a job because you don't get to work on time. Regardless of your mother's behavior in the past, you've got no one to blame if you don't do what's right today, now—in the present and in the future."

"It's time to take responsibility for your own actions," Beth said softly. "Now, Laurie, before it's too late."

Laurie lifted her eyes and looked hard at Beth and then at me. She shook her head and, with a puzzled look on her face, she said, "I guess I never thought about it like that. I really have been thinking about everything negative and forgetting the positives."

In a short while, Laurie said goodbye and went home, leaving Beth and me to wonder if anything we said would make a difference.

A few weeks later I saw Laurie again at Beth's house. I was amazed at the change in her. She walked into the room with a confident step, her head up, her eyes bright and alert. No shuffling, downcast girl anymore, she looked pretty and proud.

Even her voice was different. We had time for only a brief greeting before she left, but Beth described the metamorphosis from caterpillar to butterfly.

"Laurie has absolutely refused to discuss any past grievances. She's been trying to spend more time with her mom, and she's doing a lot more laughing. She was hired as a clerk a few weeks ago and she says the job is going well," Beth said. "She's taking a computer class and says she'll probably sign up for an accounting class next semester. Can you believe the change in that girl? Even her marriage is improving."

I've seen many people make the kind of changes Laurie made—although not many of them changed so drastically over such a short period of time. She is an exceptional young woman who, when confronted with the truth, decided not to waste any more time being miserable. A year later, she is still employed and advancing within the company. She completed the night school classes she started and plans to continue her education. Her relationship with her mother is improving daily, and she faces the challenge of marriage with a positive attitude.

Laurie chose to take full responsibility for her actions and her attitude. She decided to eliminate the negative thoughts—they served no useful, healthful purpose—and accentuate the positive factors in her life. Once she changed the direction of her attention, she saw that she had many things to celebrate. She discovered that she could enjoy life. She discovered that she could contribute to others' enjoyment of life. She discovered that she could smile.

Helen Keller wrote, "Although the world is full of suffering, it is also full of the overcoming of it."[5]

Laurie would say amen to that. She is one of the overcomers.

EXPECT THE BEST FROM PEOPLE

Expect the best from others and from yourself.

I don't think it is too large a statement to say that our expectations define us. They dictate both our attitudes and our actions. They are the expression of what we believe about life.

They will either beckon us on to accomplishment and fulfillment, or they will condemn us to despair and futility.

A young man is defined by the expectations he expresses about an encounter with a police officer. If he expects respect and orderly conduct, he probably has never been abused or mistreated by an authority figure.

A young woman is defined by the expectations she expresses about men. "They're all liars and losers... " Any doubt her life has been marked by a man who betrayed her and broke her heart?

A job applicant looks over the application form and says to himself, "I'll never get hired." It's likely his life has been characterized by failure—failure that others predicted for him.

Our expectations are programmed into us, the result of messages sent by people, experiences, and our own inner voices which are often influenced by temperament. Our expectations reveal our attitudes and dictate whether we will cower or stand in the presence of every challenge.

I'll never forget the story of Paula, a woman born with cerebral palsy. The youngest of three daughters, her older sisters never did understand that the baby of the family was different. When they got their first roller skates, they wanted Paula to have a pair. When they began riding bikes, Paula had to ride too.

Paula's handicap was mild by comparison to the some of the children she played with at the Crippled Children's Hospital, but the paralysis to her right side, her hand and leg, should have been enough to keep her off of bikes and skates. It didn't. When her sisters took piano lessons, they made room for her on the bench, and she learned to play too.

No one ever told Paula she couldn't do what her sisters did. At times, her mother was a little frightened by the activities her older children expected of their baby sister. When they climbed trees, Paula clambered up behind them. When they rode horses, she went along. When the family went target-shooting, Paula fired guns. When her father decided to add archery to the family's recreation repertoire, Paula learned to handle a bow and arrow.

In high school, Paula decided to join her sisters in the school band. She took up the French horn because, unlike the other instruments, all the finger work on the valves is done with the left hand. When her older sisters went to college, Paula made her own plans for higher education, and after graduating from high school she won a vocal scholarship.

No one ever told Paula she couldn't do what everyone else could do. No one told her she couldn't achieve. No one told her to expect achievement to be easy, however. Everything she tried had to be adapted to compensate for her weakened right side, but she never expected to fail. And no one else expected her to either.

To most people who meet her, Paula appears to live an ordinary life with her husband of twenty-four years and her two college-aged sons. But the people who are close to her know that her life is extraordinary. It has been characterized by great expectations—her own and those of her family and friends. She attempted every new experience with a solid belief that she could and would accomplish whatever she wanted to accomplish. She expected to achieve success.

If you could spend a day with Paula, riding horses with her across the vast acres she owns in Arizona, you'd find that, like the wise woman King Solomon wrote about, "She smiles at the future."[6]

Our expectations truly do define us.

When we expect the best of ourselves and others, life beckons us with an irresistible tug. We move from adventure to adventure, not without some difficulties and injuries—ask Paula how many falls she took, how many scrapes and skinned knees were required before she could skate down the street or ride a bike around the block. Disappointments were inevitable, but for Paula, they were always displaced quickly by the presence of positive expectation.

For the man and woman who have learned to expect good things, to expect success, from themselves and from others, life is flavored with the sweet taste of anticipation.

Oprah Winfrey says it this way: "When I look into the future, it's so bright it burns my eyes."[7]

Nearly fifty years have passed since I sat next to my grandfather in the crowded mezzanine of the Majestic Theater. Nearly half a century since he whispered to me in the darkness, "Things'll change someday, Thelma. Things'll change, I know it."

For African Americans of that era, the future was bleak. Our eyes burned, not with expectation, but with tears. The civil rights movement was an embryo, not yet fully formed. But Daddy Lawrence looked at the future with hope, believing that one day black people would be released from the desperate struggle simply "to be"—*to be* acknowledged as a people deserving respect and equal opportunities and equal access. Then and only then would we be allowed the opportunity to try to be the best we could be—of whatever we wanted to be.

Daddy Lawrence was right. Many things have changed. The "buzzard roost" no longer exists. The "Colored Only" signs are gone. Men and women of color are finding greater opportunities than their parents and grandparents ever experienced.

The law now mandates equal treatment for all Americans.

Legislation is in place.

We no longer need an act of Congress to ensure equality. What we need are acts of the heart and of the will—voluntary acts that demonstrate the truth we hold "self-evident, that all men are created equal."

When this truth is on display in the marketplace, in the community, in the home, then people everywhere will be able to look forward to a future so bright it burns our eyes. We will all enjoy the privilege of pursuing the dream of being the best we can be.

It is a privilege, yes, to be allowed the freedom to pursue our dreams. But never think that it is an easy pursuit. Not for anyone, of any color. Striving to be the best you can be is an everyday challenge. Booker T. Washington wrote, "Success is not to be measured by the status one has attained in life, but by the obstacles he has overcome while trying to succeed."

The jeweled bumblebee pinned to my lapel reminds me that success often looks impossible. The odds against me are great. The bumblebee should be earthbound, but it's not. An illegitimate black child born to a crippled teenager should be a ghetto statistic, but she's not. Like the ill-formed bumblebee, ungainly and unfit for flight, the chances of my getting lift-off looked small.

No one in 1941, looking down into the face of a tiny, black infant girl would have prophesied, "This child will one day own her own company and travel the world, speaking and teaching people about being the best they can be."

No one, except Daddy Lawrence and Grannie and Daddy Harrell. Oh, they didn't see the specifics of my life, but they did see my value as a human being. And they invested in me, believing with all their hearts that I was valuable.

Becoming the best you can be is never a solitary accomplishment. For every man and woman who achieves, there are many others who believed in them, who valued them and invested in them to help make their success a reality. These investors are seldom the subject of Oscar-winning movies. Their stories are seldom told, their heroic sacrifices seldom heralded, but they too are examples of great success. Theirs are achievements of the heart, and unlike business or athletic or artistic success, nothing can undo their accomplishments: not business reverses, not economic downturns, nor injuries or natural disasters. Theirs is the example that each of us should follow. Because success, true success, is never selfish.

No one is a better example of that fact than Mary McLeod Bethune. The daughter of former slaves, the youngest of fifteen children, Mary McLeod Bethune grew up during the final years of black reconstruction. Widely educated, Bethune was the only black student of her class when she graduated from Chicago's Moody Bible Institute in 1895. An educator and writer, she was a tireless scholar, but her dreams of success didn't end with an assortment of academic degrees, of which she had many. She wanted more than awards for writing and teaching. She wanted to invest herself in the lives of others.

With a dream and a few coins, Mary bought a piece of land called "Hell's Hole," and embarked on a venture to build a small house-school into a college. The Normal and Industrial School for Negro Girls was later named Bethune-Cookman College and became a respected institution for higher learning. Before her death in 1955, Mary McLeod Bethune not only served for many years the college she had founded, passionately investing herself in the lives of Negro Americans, but she went on to found the National Council of Negro Women and served as the director of the Division of Negro Affairs for President Roosevelt's Administration.[8]

Mary McLeod Bethune wrote, "Invest in the human soul. Who knows, it might be a diamond in the rough."[9]

Her life was a vivid expression of her words and a challenge to all of us who aspire to achieve.

As we pursue our dreams of success, as we set out to be the best that we can be, let us remember that unless we invest in others, our success will never be complete.

No matter how large a pile of treasures we may be able to accumulate, no matter how rich our coffers, no matter how famous our faces and how lauded our feats, unless we have stored riches that cannot be lost—riches of the spirit—our success will be inadequate and insufficient.

In the final analysis, unless our search for success includes a passionate search for diamonds in the rough, for people whose lives we can invest in, our portfolio, no matter how impressive, will be lacking. Our efforts at being the best we can be will fall far short.

I think Simone de Beauvoir, the French writer and philosopher said it well: "One's life has value so long as one attributes value to the life of others, by means of love, friendship, indignation and compassion."[10]

As fine a quote as that is, I think Althea Hilliard's

paraphrase is even more powerful. "You do what's right, Thelma, 'cause I'll be watching!" she shouted.

From the sidewalk of a now-buried neighborhood, a woman proclaimed that I had value, that I was worth protecting, that my life counted for something. Who was I, a mere child, to argue with her?

Althea's voice has followed me all my life, reminding me that achievement is not solitary.

Grannie's voice reminds me daily that, if God is in it, He will make the way.

Daddy Lawrence, his husky voice a clear memory, whispers down through the years: Have hope, Thelma. Have hope.

Their voices convinced me that, no matter how unlikely my circumstances, no matter how ungainly my form, I didn't have to be earthbound. I, like the bumblebee, could get lift-off, in spite of the odds against it.

If I had a megaphone now instead of ink and paper, I'd shout it loudly, so that everyone could hear: Your life matters! God is able! Don't give up!

If the metaphor of the bumblebee has any significance, it is this: Don't believe the lie that you can't fly.

You *can* be the best of whatever you want to "bee!"

ENDNOTES

1. Jansen, Dan, and McCallum, Jack, *Full Circle,* Villard Books (New York, 1994) p. 161
2. Ibid., 177
3. Ibid., 179
4. Matthew 5:9
5. Fitzhenry, Robert I., Editor, *The Harper Book of Quotations* (New York City: Harper Collins, 1993) p. 1
6. Proverbs 31:25b (NASV)
7. *The Quotable Woman* (Philadelphia: Running Press, 1991) p. 21
8. Salley, Columbus, *The Black 100* (New York: Citadel Press, Carol Publishing Group) 1994, p. 324-325
9. *The Quotable Woman* (Philadelphia: Running Press, 1991) p. 180
10. Ibid., 60